Operation Exodus II

Answers You Need To know
About Explosive Future Events

Steve Lightle
copyright © 1998
All Rights Reserved

Operation Exodus II
ANSWERS YOU NEED TO KNOW ABOUT
EXPLOSIVE FUTURE EVENTS
ISBN:1-890900-05-2
Copyright © 1998 by Steve Lightle
P. O. Box 70069
Bellevue, WA 98007-0069

Published by:
Insight Publishing
8801 South Yale Suite 410
Tulsa, OK 74137

Another Book by this Author
EXODUS II
Let My people Go!

Printed in the U.S.A.

CONTENTS

PREFACE

DAILY I'M LOADED

After writing *Exodus II* in 1983, many people asked for an update about the return of the Soviet Jews to Israel. Writing about prophetic events puts one on a tight rope and indeed it should, so that the author repeats only what the Lord gives.

Writing a book is a great task, especially for me. The words of Ecclesiastes 12:12 come to me each time I go into a book store. "And further, my son, be admonished by these. Of making many books there is no end, and much study is wearisome to the flesh." So the Lord had to make it very clear to write another book. I have even procrastinated in writing it for a number of reasons. Then came inspiration from the Holy Spirit.

There were some people who thought I had fallen out of a tree and landed on my head when *Exodus II* was published. How could one of the strongest nations ever on the face of the earth cough up the Jewish people behind its borders and allow them to go to Israel? Many said it would never come to pass. I was simply the messenger. As the professor of Old Testament History of Elim Bible College in London, England said, "If it comes to pass, then we will know Steve heard from God." He spoke this at a conference in Brussels, Belgium in 1984 where we were both speakers. He continued, "If it does not come to pass, then he did not hear from God."

When the Soviet Union disintegrated before our very eyes, the Iron Curtain came down and the Berlin Wall was demolished. The Jewish people from the former USSR began going to Israel in unprecedented numbers. At the writing of this book, over 900,000 have gone to Israel since 1990. To God be the glory.

I was invited to speak to a Messianic congregation in Israel in 1990. When the pastor introduced me to his congregation he first asked for my forgiveness. I was so surprised, because I had known him since 1975. The reason he asked for my forgiveness was because he had never believed that the Jews would ever come out of Russia. Of course, I forgave him. Then he pointed out to me the 150 people wearing earphones that morning. He said those were Russian Jews now in his congregation receiving translation from Hebrew to Russian. He apologized for not believing or praying about this exodus.

When hundreds of thousands of Jews went to Israel from the USSR, people realized that I had not landed on my head.

Some Christians have cast away Israel from having anything to do with the end times. And consider quite preposterous the idea that the return of the Jewish people to Israel will result in the greatest evangelistic harvest the world has ever known. This time God will replace those who hold these views.

But to many, I believe this book will be a blessing.

I have been asked on a number of occasions if I had ever doubted that the Jews from the former Soviet Union would go to Israel. My answer was always, "NO!" because, "Blessed be the LORD, who daily loads us with benefits, the God of our salvation! Selah" (Psalm 68:19). The Lord assured me daily and loaded me with His presence.

Likewise, He has done the same thing concerning this book.

My purpose for writing this book is in no way to establish patterns of any kind to be followed in prayer warfare. Therefore, the reader is cautioned to be very careful not to copy the prayer journeys told about in this book. However, I do pray the reader will be encouraged to pray more and seek the Lord more and more.

God never goes about what He is doing in the same way twice. Just as is recorded in 2 Samuel 5, David stopped to inquire of the Lord for His directions to battle the Philistines. After defeating them, the Philistines with the same army in the same valley tried to battle David's army in the same way a second time. But again, David inquired of the Lord to get His battle plan. David did not trust in his victories or successes. David trusted in the Lord. We must do the same. The Lord gave him a different plan to defeat the Philistines a second time.

Therefore, do not copy others in spiritual warfare. The sons of Sceva did in Acts 19:13-16. And they fled naked and wounded.

"'Therefore behold, I am against the prophets,' says the Lord, 'who steal My words every one from his neighbor'" (Jeremiah 23:30).

I encourage you to seek the Lord and ask Him what and how to pray about a matter, and He will give you His plan. It will not be the same as told in this book or by others.

Steve Lightle

DEDICATION

To the Jewish people throughout the
world and their making aliyah to Israel.

Baruch Ben Barak

ACKNOWLEDGEMENTS

Writing does not come easy for me, but with the Lord's help, it is finished. I want to thank the Lord Jesus for inspiring me to write this book.

To my wife, Judy, goes my love and affection. I call her "My Glory" based on I Corinthians 11:7. She helps me keep my two feet on the ground. I am so blessed to have a family that accepts me the way I am. Thanks to my daughters Lynn and Michele and their families.

Without Naomi Mathews there would be no manuscript. Her typing and editing have helped me dearly. She constantly amazed me with her skills at the computer, with the English language, and being able to decipher my notes on the pages. Thank you, Naomi. Also to her husband, Larry, for serving up great lunches and removing snow from my car so many times.

I remember my dad telling me when I was a youngster, "If you make one good friend in life, you will be fortunate. If you make more, you will indeed be blessed." Well, I am blessed many times over. My thanks to Bob and Ann Wooldridge, and to Glen and Anne Wooldridge, for providing me "Bob's" office for many weeks at Wooldridge Boat Company in Seattle, to write this book.

I also thank Angelo and Therese Borrelli for having "room at the inn" when I met with Naomi during the book editing process.

I give special thanks to the intercessors who have prayed for me and encouraged me and given finances to see this work completed.

CHAPTER 1
BOMBS AWAY

It was about five o'clock on a beautiful early morning in August 1979. My wife Judy, daughter Michele, and I were standing at the top of the Mount of Olives. There was a quiet expectation in each of us as we waited to see Jerusalem as "The City of Gold".

The sky was dark blue as streams of light began to invade the darkness of night that was now quickly diminishing. A beautiful song, "Jerusalem, City of Gold" was running through my mind. This song was written concerning this time of the morning in Jerusalem. As the first rays of sun begin to shine upon the buildings made of Jerusalem stones, they look like gold. We wanted to experience this sight, which was why we were at the top of the Mount of Olives at such an early hour.

On our way to the Mount of Olives, we had first stopped to pick up Joy, a friend of our other daughter, Lynn. Lynn, Joy, and our friend Matt were on the back side of what was then the Intercontinental Hotel, and were playing tennis there on a large court.

Judy, Michele, and I had walked toward the edge of the Mount of Olives that overlooks the city of

Jerusalem from a vantage point. As we walked along, suddenly, about twelve feet in front of us, a tremendous explosion blew part of the wall completely away. Immediately after this explosion, the three of us who were walking together screamed out the name of Jesus. We were completely protected; not one of us was hurt. It was a very frightening experience as this was a considerably large explosion. Rocks catapulted from the wall, sailing directly over our heads. The rocks then flew over the Intercontinental Hotel, over the top of the Mount of Olives, finally landing on the court where Lynn, Joy, and Matt were playing tennis. They had to run quickly for cover, as this shower of rocks was falling all around them.

This fearful experience traumatized our daughter, Michele. The only thing she could think of concerning Israel following this incident was about the bomb that had exploded so close to us. This was the first time I had taken my family with me to Israel. I knew this was Satan's attempt at discouraging us from fulfilling what God would ask us to do at a later time.

In 1981, Judy and I felt very impressed that we were to move to Israel. So we did. However, Michele was vehemently opposed to going to Israel again, most especially to living there. Clearly, the memory of the bomb exploding at the Mount of Olives two years earlier was still very fresh in her mind.

Nevertheless, the time did come, when Judy and I were living in the city of Jerusalem, that Michele and Lynn joined us. This proved to be a very difficult time for Michele, especially at first. However, Satan always overplays his hand by going too far, exposing himself. This, however, is an opportunity for God's grace to intervene, so His divine will can be accomplished in our lives.

1 Corinthians 2:8 says, that if Satan and all of his demons had understood the mysteries of God, they would never have crucified the Lord of Glory. Satan always oversteps his bounds.

After 1974, when God by His grace allowed me to see the vision of the release of the Jewish people out of the Soviet Union and their return to Israel, I made numerous trips to the former Soviet Union. In 1983, I was very much impressed by the Holy Spirit to take my wife and Michele with me on my next trip.

When I proposed this trip to Judy and Michele, immediately Michele said, "No, Dad. I am not going!" She absolutely refused.

So I said to her, "Well, Michele, won't you just pray about it?"

She quickly answered, "No! I won't pray about it!"

I asked her why, and she replied, "Because, if I pray about it, I'm sure Jesus is going to tell me I have to go. So, I'm not even going to pray about it."

At this time, Michele was fourteen years old and was usually a very happy and joyful young girl. But now, she simply walked away from me and went into her room. About twenty minutes later she came back out, a totally different girl.

She casually said, "Oh, by the way, when are we going to Russia, Dad?"

Surprised, I replied, "Excuse me? I thought you said you weren't going to go."

To which she replied, "Oh, when I was in my room the Lord reminded me of the time we stood on the top of the Mount of Olives. When that bomb went off, not even one speck of dust got on me. We were standing so close to that explosion, yet nothing happened to us. If God can take care of me there," she continued, "He can certainly take care of me in the Soviet Union. So when are we going?"

Through the power and anointing of the Holy Spirit, it was bombs away! Our daughter suffered no ill effects of that explosion ever again. Further, she had no problems concerning living in Israel after that. She also went to the Soviet Union with Judy and me. In fact, it was through Michele that the Lord did some miraculous things that very possibly saved us from being placed into some very difficult situations.

I had complete confidence in Michele that she had heard the voice of the Lord. She confirmed what the Lord had said to me.

The Lord trains us to hear His voice so that He can lead us by His Holy Spirit. This is one of the ways we know we are His sons (Romans 8:14).

I remember one such experience I had while speaking at a large conference in Hameenlinna, a city in central Finland. One day, Keiijo was given the task of driving me into town. I wanted to buy a pair of Finnish sandals, which are very comfortable. It was late in July, but the shoe stores no longer sold sandals. Not discouraged, I prayed and asked the Lord what to do. The Lord's reply to me was to buy Keiijo the best pair of shoes possible.

Keiijo was one of the coworkers from a Bible school, and had a horrible looking pair of shoes on. I said, "Keiijo, what is the best pair of shoes in the store?" He showed me the pair of shoes. I asked him to try them on to see if I liked the looks of them on someone else. He obliged. I asked him if they felt good and were comfortable. He said, "I have never even tried on such a pair, let alone own such shoes." When I told him not to take them off, that they were his, he began to cry. I hadn't meant to embarrass him. Keiijo then went on to tell me how the week before, while preaching the gospel in Poland, he noticed that his interpreter's shoes were held together with string. On seeing this, he gave his shoes to him. The only other pair of shoes Keiijo owned were those with the holes he was wearing that day.

Then Keiijo asked me, "How did you know it was my birthday today?"

I simply replied, "I didn't, but Jesus did!" So we both cried.

Dear ones, obey the voice of the Lord.

CHAPTER 2
THE GREAT POTATO PARTY

During the summer of 1983, Judy, Michele, and I were in Finland attending a conference near Helsinki where I was speaking. It was the beginning of God moving in a very spiritual way in Michele's heart and life.

God did a fresh work in Michele's life at that time. We were preparing to make our trip into the Soviet Union—to Leningrad, today called St. Petersburg—and to Minsk, which is the capital of Bellarus. We went to the travel agent's office that I used in Helsinki to apply for the visas, hotel bookings, and flights for my various trips into the USSR. We had no problem getting into Leningrad; however, he said it was not possible for us to go to Minsk. I knew after praying about it that Minsk was a place we were supposed to go. Bo, the travel agent, had the representative from Intourist on the telephone, which was the Soviet Agency that handled all the bookings for foreigners coming into the USSR.

While talking, he covered the phone, turned to Judy and me and asked, "Have you ever had anything to do with potatoes?"

We asked him, "Potatoes? What do potatoes have to do with Minsk?"

He replied, "Well, they are just telling me that the International Potato Exposition will be held in the city of Minsk. This is right during the time you want to go there. Because of that, all the hotels are full and the flights are all booked. But maybe if you know something about potatoes we might be able to get you there."

Judy spoke up and said, "Well, we owned a restaurant for seven and a half years and we cooked a lot of French fries."

Bo spoke into the phone again and said, "Yes, these people have been experts in potatoes for some years."

It is interesting that every time God asks you to do something, many things will try to discourage you and the enemy will try to block you, even make it seem impossible. However, we must persevere when we know the Lord has said to go and do an assignment.

As our airplane approached the city of Minsk in August 1983, Michele was sitting next to the window and I was sitting beside her. Judy was in the row behind us.

Michele turned to me and said, "Dad, we're going to be followed by women KGB agents here."

I looked at her and asked, "Michele, how do you know that?"

She replied, "Because my heart is beating and I know it is Jesus who is speaking to me and He told me to tell you this."

So I just said, "Okay," remembering Isaiah 11:6b, ". . . a little child shall lead them."

So in this fresh work that God was doing in Michele's life, the Lord released the gifts of the Spirit. She was used with the discerning of spirits in a wonderful way according to 1 Corinthians 12:10.

When this trip happened it was almost enough to laugh about, because here we were sent, the three of us. We were given seats on the airplanes, we were given hotel space, and we were given official documents to attend the Potato Exposition.

So God made a way where there was no way.

God dealt with His enemy, and I must not let my enemy stop me from carrying out the assignments God gives me. I learned a very valuable lesson here. God has no enemies. None. Not one. God is so great He has no enemies and that is why He can sit in heaven and laugh. Jesus totally exposed all the works of the Devil. He totally stripped him of his power and his authority. That is why in 1 Peter 5:8, Peter says, ". . .your adversary, the Devil. . ." Not God's adversary. He's your adversary; he's my adversary. When we come to know who we are in God and are seated in heavenly places in Christ Jesus (Ephesians 2:6), we can look down at our circumstances and then begin to laugh as He does (Psalm 2:4).

Michele identified every KGB agent who was trailing us. On one occasion she said,

"Dad, do you see the lady in the green dress?"

I answered, "Yes."

She said, "She is one of them."

I replied, "Really? How do you know, Michele?"

She replied, "Dad, my heart is burning inside me and Jesus is speaking to me right now. Jesus said, 'That's one'."

We would then proceed to do evasive things, and sure enough she was. Then, when that agent knew we were aware that she was following us, she would be gone. Soon, another agent would begin to follow us and Michele would say, "Dad, there is another one." In a short time we went through all the agents they had assigned to us.

We then stopped so none of our contacts would be jeopardized. As we sat on a certain park bench, one of these agents—a lady who had been following us—came and sat on another bench directly across the path from us. She was pretending to read a book, but was staring at us.

Michele looked at me and said, "Dad, this is the greatest adventure I've ever been on in my life. You go that way, I'll go this way, we'll send Mother the other way and we will really confuse them." Then the three of us started to laugh.

Some time later, after going to an apartment to contact Jewish people, we began to return toward our hotel. We stopped to rest as we had been out for many hours, and were sitting on a bench in the middle of a very large sidewalk beside a wide street. Walking toward us were two police officers in full uniform.

Now, I had been written up by *TASS* News Agency earlier that year. *TASS* gave me a full-page editorial and the headline read: GOD BRINGS RUSSIA TO HER KNEES. That headline was the only good thing in the entire article. This particular article reported on something I had shared in Finland concerning the exodus of the Jewish people and *TASS* ridiculed it. A photographer proceeded to take about seven rolls of pictures of me there.

I asked my interpreter, "Hey, who is that guy? He's taking too many pictures."

My interpreter replied, "Oh, didn't anybody tell you that he's the photographer for *TASS*?"

So I smiled, as I wanted them to have a good picture of me when it hit the desk of the KGB. Evidently they wanted to remember me.

So here came these two police officers and while they were approaching us, I happened to look up. One of them looked at me and evidently recognized me because he pointed toward me. He then went to great lengths to pretend he didn't see me. First, he began to speak into his Walkie Talkie. Then the two of them made a full circle around us, about ten to twelve feet away, pretending they didn't see us. Next, a police van drove up with police officers and plainclothesmen in it, about twenty men in all. They began to circle us as well, all of them pretending not to see us.

We were just sitting there watching all of this, when suddenly I burst out laughing. I mean, I had a belly roller.

Judy said, "Steven, I don't think this is the time to laugh."

I replied, "I can't help it."

She asked, "Why not?"

At that moment the Lord brought a scripture verse to my mind. It was a portion of James 2:19 that says, the devils know there is a God and they are trembling.

So I said to Judy, "Look who's afraid. Here is a teenager, a housewife, and Dippy Duck (I used to own a business called Dippy Duck Car Wash). And look at that, it takes twenty of them to decide how to handle three seemingly insignificant believers in God. That's enough to cause you to laugh, because they are the ones shaking. They are the ones who are afraid. In Daniel 11:32 it says, '. . . those who know their God shall be strong and do exploits . . .'"

And because "He who is in you is greater than he who is in the world" (1 John 4:4), we stood up and walked right through the midst of them and continued to walk until we got back to our hotel.

It was such a blessing to see how the Lord ministered to Judy and me through Michele.

The reason why we were in the Soviet Union had begun nine years before. I was in the city of Braunschweig, West Germany, in August of 1974. I had such a desire in my heart to understand more of certain scriptures I had read.

I went into a room in a building called the "Koffeetweeta". This was a ministry where drug addicts were being cared for. My wife and I had lived in this building in 1973 with our family. We were helping drug addicts and alcoholics recover from these terrible addictions. There was a little chamber where we could go to pray that was situated on the fourth floor.

On a certain day, I went to this chamber and said, "Jesus, either I am going to die in this room, or you are going to change my life." As soon as I had closed the door and turned around, the power of God hit me and I fell flat on my face. I did not get off the floor for six and one-half days. I couldn't sit in a chair; I couldn't stand up. But I recognized God was in the room. I knew there was somebody standing in a corner of the room, then there was someone else standing in the opposite corner. God opened my spiritual eyes to see into the unseen realm.

When I opened my eyes and looked into the corner, a creature was standing there whose belt buckle was about twenty-five feet high. The room was about twenty to twenty-two feet high, and he was taller than that. Angels do not have to conform to the dimensions of this world. It was incredible. He was so large, and he had six wings. He looked in every direction and yet he did not move. I had such an assurance in my heart that God had placed him there for my protection.

Then I looked in the opposite corner and there was another angel standing there. I knew for certain that God had brought me to this place for a divine appointment.

I cannot tell all of the things that happened in those six and one-half days. Some things are not right for man to even speak of. But God in His grace sent three people to see me. One man came in, opened the door, and fell flat on the floor and said,

"Oh, I can't even breathe in this place!" So he crawled out and slammed the door.

I said, "Thank you Jesus, I'm certainly not hallucinating."

The next man came in and said, "What's going on in this place?" He sat in a chair for about twenty minutes and then he had to leave. A third man, Phil Israelson, came in and said, "God is in this place." He spent two and one-half days on the floor with me in this room. I wish I'd had a camera when God opened Phil's spiritual eyes. I would have won any photo contest when Phil looked in the corner; his eyes looked like two sunny-side-up eggs.

I said, "Philip, what do you see?"

He said, "Oh, I don't know."

I said, "Just explain to me, did you see something?" I was acting very nonchalant. He then described to me exactly what I had seen.

I said, "Well, look around the room."

And he said "Oh! There's another one right there."

We had quite an experience in that room.

Phil had to leave after two and a half days, and toward the end of the six and a half days, I was still lying on the floor. My head was resting on my arm. I had cried all the tears that were within me. There was not another drop of water. I couldn't cry anymore, I couldn't do anything.

Then I heard the voice of someone standing by me say, "I want you to trust me."

I replied, "Lord, I trust you."

He said, "I want you to trust me."

I said, "Lord, I trust you."

He said, "You have to trust me."

So I knew it was something very serious. I lifted my head off of my arm and looked, and Jesus was standing there with an axe in His hand.

Then I understood why I had to trust Him. Jesus took that axe and began to lay it into things that were in my heart which did not belong there.

It was a precious time of being with Jesus. I got up and was finally able to sit in a big overstuffed chair. Suddenly, the entire wall in front of me became like a movie screen, a theater in cinemascope. And I began to see faces. Jewish faces. I saw multitudes of Jewish faces. Hundreds of thousands of Jewish faces. Then

God let me see the nation they were in. They were in the Soviet Union. God spoke to me and told me there would be those who would be raised up to go to the authorities of the Soviet Union and say, "Thus saith the Lord God of Israel. Let my people go." The authorities would not let them go, and God, through these men, would begin to prophesy to the USSR.

Next, I began to see these highways, and I saw the Jewish people begin to come out. They boarded ships and went to Israel.

I said, "Lord, that is wonderful! But what has that got to do with me?"

And the Lord said, "Son, you are to go to Jewish communities within the Soviet Union and tell them that I am going to deliver them with an exodus that will be greater than the exodus out of Egypt. I am going to bring them back home to Israel. Go and prepare the way."

I said, "Lord, that isn't the most popular thing to do today."

The Lord said, "I will be with you."

I said, "If You are with me, show me this in the Word."

If the Word is not the basis of everything that God does in your life, forget it. Throw it away. Do not submit to it. Have nothing to do with it. It is the Word and only the Word that is our basis and our authority. There is no prophecy, there is no vision, there is nothing that God is going to do outside of His Word.

As I began to read Jeremiah 23, God gave me an illumination of His Word. And as the revelation started to come forth, I began to understand something of what God's plan was. The book, *EXODUS II*, tells this in more detail.

CHAPTER 3
THE 4 SMITHSKIS

Gates are mentioned many times in the scriptures. They are important because whoever holds the gates of a city controls what happens within that city. We have a promise that God gave to Abraham in Genesis 22:17 that his seed would possess the gate of his enemies. Jesus said in Matthew 16:18, the gates of hell shall not prevail against His church.

One reason Nehemiah was so sad after he inquired about his brethren in the city of Jerusalem, was that he was told the gates had been burned with fire (Nehemiah 1:3). This disturbed Nehemiah very much. He understood that without any gates there was no authority or protection for the city. Any band of marauding gangs or enemies could come and plunder the city at will and do to it whatever they wished.

Judges 16:1-3 tells the story of Samson at Gaza and how he crippled the city in the middle of the night. Samson took the gates of the city, the posts that the gates sat upon, and the cross bar as well. He packed them on his back and went up to the top of a hill toward an area that overlooked Hebron. It must have been a very fearful thing for the people of Gaza to wake up the next morning and find the protection of their city had been totally removed.

Joshua 20:4 tells us that the elders sat at the gate of the city.

After Sarah died, Abraham went to buy the piece of ground at Machpelah. He went to the gate of the city of Hebron. Genesis 23:19 tells why Abraham bought his piece of property there. It was because that was where the elders sat and conducted business so that others could see what was being done. It was a place where judges would sit conducting court.

As related in Ruth 4:1-2, Boaz went to inquire about redeeming Ruth because he was a near kinsman. He went to the gate of the city to take care of this matter.

In Isaiah 26:2, the scripture commands, "Open the gates, that the righteous nation which keeps the truth may enter in." According to the Apostle Paul in Romans 3:1-2, the Jewish nation was entrusted to keep the oracles of God. The reason we have the Old Testament today is that the Jews were faithful to keep the scriptures. They wrote them down to pass them on. Had they not done this there would not be an Old Testament. God is saying that the gates must be opened for the Jewish people to go to Israel.

In 1985 after many months of preparation, the Lord had prepared four of us—Johannes Facius, Phil Israelson, Matt McLallin, and me—to make this trip into the Soviet Union. We were to go through the gates of various cities, just as is proclaimed in Isaiah 62:10. "Go through, go through the gates! Prepare the way for the people; build up, build up, the highway! Take out the stones, lift up a banner for the peoples!"

We made the trip into the Soviet Union to open the gates to the various cities which had significant Jewish populations. This trip was made so that at the set time, the Jewish people would be allowed to leave those areas. We were simply to go to the gates of those cities and in prayer cooperate with God, prepare the way for the people, and remove stones out of their way. By prayer a banner was placed on the gates so that the Jewish people would be able to immigrate to the nation of Israel.

We applied for and received Soviet permission, by Divine intervention, to go to the major cities from which I saw the Jewish people leaving in the vision the Lord gave me in 1974.

One strategy the four of us used to make this trip is contained in Zechariah 1:18-21. It says that there were four horns who had scattered Judah, Israel, and Jerusalem. It also says that the Lord wanted to raise up four craftsmen, carpenters, or blacksmiths. The word in Hebrew could mean any one of those. So we called ourselves "blacksmiths". We decided that we would have a code name; we were the "Four Smithskis".

Johannes was Johanneski. Phil was Philski, Matt was Mattski, and I was Steveski. So, as the "Four Smithskis", we went to carry out Zechariah 1:21. There it says that these blacksmiths were going to terrify the four horns of the nations that lifted up their hands against the land of Judah and scattered it.

Undeniably, the Jewish people in the Soviet Union had been scattered a long way from Judah.

As the Russian train pulled into the station in Volgograd, a large city in the USSR, I began to wonder how God would let the Jewish community here know about their upcoming exodus back to Israel. Looking for the gates to the city, the Four Smithskis prepared to get off the train. My thoughts turned to how the enemy would try to thwart us. Then I remembered Ephesians 6:12: "For we do not wrestle against flesh and blood, but against principalities, against powers, against the rulers of the darkness of this age, against spiritual hosts of wickedness in the heavenly places." This helped me to keep focused, because we do not wrestle against people.

In all my travels in the Soviet Union, I was constantly followed by the KGB. The Soviet Jews referred to them as "Shh! One, two, three," meaning KGB. But the KGB were only pawns of the real enemies, the ones your natural eye cannot see. They are the ones we battle. Sometimes the KGB would set up elaborate schemes to keep us from meeting any Soviet Jews and from letting us know that they were following us.

When we arrived at the Volgograd train station, we were met by our "guide", often times spelled "KGB".

The first words out of our "guide's" mouth were, "We have arranged a meeting for you tonight."

I said to her, "That's interesting; you arranged a meeting for us tonight?"

"Yes, we're taking you to the English Club at the university here," she answered.

I said, "Well, really?"

She then went on to say, "Yes, we always do this. When French speaking people come, we take them to the French Club. When English speaking people come we take them to the English Club. Therefore, we have set up a meeting for you with the English Club tonight."

I knew immediately it was a trap. The first thing they wanted to do was to take us somewhere to keep us busy so we couldn't contact any Jewish people. However, to my amazement, the Lord witnessed to me, "You go with them." I thought, "Oh, joy!" The other three Smithskis confirmed that this was indeed a trap, but they also agreed that we should go.

About an hour after we had arrived in Volgograd we left our hotel in a taxi arranged for us by our "guide". The taxi driver drove and drove and drove until he had left the city. This was outside the area our visas allowed. He finally turned off to an unpaved road. The mud in the road was very deep and we went far into the woods, "somewhere". Then behold, there was this one little building, all by itself, just a little place.

I thought, "Oh sure, this is where the English Club from the university meets." We were way out in the middle of nowhere. Something like this had never happened to us on previous trips to the Soviet Union. Surprisingly, the president of the English Club came out of this little building to greet us and ushered us in. We were with this English Club until exactly eight o'clock in the evening. Suddenly, as they were interrogating us, they stopped right in the middle of what they were doing.

They just stood up and said, "It's all over, good-bye, see you later."

We said, "What do you mean, goodbye?"

They replied, "We have done what we were told to do. We have never done this before."

I thought, isn't this interesting? Our "guide" told us they have these meetings often. These university students were forced to hold this meeting just for us, to keep us occupied so that we couldn't contact Soviet Jews.

What intricate moves they had contrived for us. The president of the English Club then said,

"Now you have to leave and go back to your hotel."

So I asked, "How will we get back to our hotel?"

He simply replied, "That's your problem."

So I questioned him and asked, "What do you mean, it's our problem?"

His reply was, "Well, go out there and wait for a taxi."

Not quite believing him I said, "A taxi? There will never be a taxi out here in the middle of the woods."

So he said, "All right, I'll come and stand out there with you and maybe we will find somebody who will take you back to your hotel."

We stood out in the cold, all but sinking away in the mud. It was an absolute terrible mess. Incredibly, after some time, along came a car. The president flagged down the man and handed him a couple of rubles, then said to us, "This man will take you to your hotel." So the four of us got into the man's car. The driver was a great big man with a wonderful smile on his face, and he began to speak to us in Russian. However, we couldn't speak Russian so we replied to him in English, but he couldn't understand us.

Johannes tried to speak to the driver in Danish and, of course, he couldn't understand Danish either. Then Johannes and I both tried German, with no response from the driver. We all began to wonder how we could ever communicate with this man, when suddenly he turned around, looked at me and said, "Ahta mid-a-bear Evrit?" which in Hebrew means, "Do you speak Hebrew?" I about fell out of the car! I thought, what is this? The authorities go through an elaborate process to keep us from the Soviet Jewish community. Yet, our driver turns out to be the head man of the entire Jewish community in Volgograd. God had delivered us right into his car!

We began to speak to each other in Hebrew, and the driver said, "Please, can I show you around our city?"

So he took us on a little tour and showed us where the synagogue used to be. There was no synagogue there anymore; the Communists had closed it. The driver then explained to us, "When the Jewish people celebrate their various feasts, Passover, for instance, they need matzo bread. They had to get it from Kiev, a long way away."

Then he asked, "Can I take you to my brother's apartment where my brother's family and I can talk with you?"

Our answer was, "Of course."

We talked with them until the wee hours of the morning. After being there most of the night, it was time to go back to our hotel.

I shall never forget this man and his brother. As they stood next to the car, tears streaming down their faces, they asked, "Is there any way we could go to Israel with you?" It was impossible in the natural to take them. I mean, my pocket wasn't big enough for them. However, I would take them out in my prayers. I looked forward to the day when I would get to see that family in Israel.

We got into the car again and he took us to within two blocks of the hotel and let us out there. We certainly knew that there would be people looking for us. After all, we hadn't been in our beds all night; I could just imagine the fuming that was going on inside the KGB and inside our "guide's" mind.

Our disappearance had caused a minor stir. We were asked many times where we had been. Our answer was simply, "We were sent by you out to the middle of nowhere and it took us this long to get back."

Our primary task was to build the highway God had shown me in the vision in Germany. It is a highway built by God through prayer. It is more real than concrete. It is something established and built in the spirit. It is there, on location. I have had people ask me, "Why do you have to go to the Soviet Union and pray? How are you going to build a highway when you can't even work a bulldozer? This is a little ridiculous, don't you think? Couldn't you just take a map of the Soviet Union and move your finger across it and as you do, pray? That would be good enough, wouldn't it?"

No. It would not be good enough, because one principle of intercession is identification. What if Jesus had stayed in Heaven and just prayed for you and never came to earth? However, He did come and He identified with us. He was then able to win the victory. Jesus identified with you because He came as a man. You also can have the victory and help others through prayer.

Identification is very important. If it is at all possible, go to the place and pray. We went to prophetically prepare the way. Ninety percent of the Jewish people in the Soviet Union lived in major metropolitan areas. As we would find the ancient gates of the cities, we would go through them. Then, "It would be recorded in heaven," as Philski would say, so the Jews could leave.

We had some very interesting things happen, especially with the KGB following us. They just couldn't understand what we were doing. We did some very peculiar things.

For instance, in the city of Odessa, there is a giant set of steps that go down to the Black Sea. They are called the Potemkin Staircase, and are very impressive. They extend from the square where the opera house is located, down to the harbor. Our guide told us that this was the ancient gate to the city.

To which we responded, "Thank you, we don't need any more of the tour." We had found the place we had wanted to find.

Our assignment was to terrorize the four horns that had scattered the children of Israel from Jerusalem and Judah who were still being held at the four corners of the earth. Recognizing that God had placed the anointing of His Spirit upon us, we returned later and lined ourselves up across these steps. We needed to identify the idols in order to terrorize them. It was incredible.

As we marched in line down the flight of steps, the Lord just told us to pray aloud in the Holy Spirit. When at the bottom, we were to simply turn around, walk back up the stairs and return to our hotel. Our assignment would then be completed.

Now we know from the Bible that the elders of Israel always sat in the gates of the cities. However, they gave up their position, and the demonic powers moved in. These powers began to control the gates so that they could control the cities. Therefore, prophetically, the Lord made us go through those gates in order to terrorize the demonic powers, and to make a highway for the Jewish people to get to Israel.

When we got down to the bottom of those steps in Odessa, we turned around to start back up. There were two members of the KGB following right behind us and when our abrupt turn caught them off guard, their faces turned bright red. They looked like little boys caught with their hands in the cookie jar, not knowing what to do next. You never saw anybody so fearful in your life.

They turned and just ran as fast as they could up the stairs. We often wondered what they reported back to their headquarters.

"What did those men do?"

"Well, they walked to the bottom of the steps, turned around and walked back up, then went to their hotel."

"Really? And what did you do?"

"Well, we ran, we got out of there."

They are probably still trying to figure out what languages were being spoken that day.

Traveling across the Soviet Union was interesting. We flew in from Japan into the city of Khabarovsk, in Far East Russia. From the very beginning of the trip as we traveled to the gates of the different cities, we were attended by the presence of the Lord in a very precious way. I'm sure the angels were also with us. God simply commanded us to go to the gates of the cities and He would do the rest of the work. We repeatedly saw how our guides always managed to find the gates to the cities. Some gates were physically still there, while others had been destroyed through the centuries.

Some years later, I had tears streaming down my face the day Natan Sharansky, the most well known

"Prisoner of Conscience and Refusenik", arrived in Israel. A group of us in Jerusalem watched the television coverage of Sharansky's arrival. Sharansky's wife, who had fought for years for his release from prison in the Soviet Union, made this statement. "Let this be but the first of all the rest that have yet to come."

My involvement began in 1974, when God by His grace allowed me to see a vision of the release of the Soviet Jews. Since then, I have either publicly or privately been working to see this truly happen. As wonderful as it was for Mr. Sharansky to return to Israel, together with many other Jewish people, it is God's plan to announce an even greater return. All of this points to the fact that there is another One coming. Jeremiah refers to Him as the "Lord Our Righteousness" in Jeremiah chapter 23.

The focal point is the coming of the Messiah. He will return again, not as a lamb led to the slaughter, but as the King of Kings, the Lord of Lords, the Lion of the tribe of Judah.

CHAPTER 4

ONE PICTURE IS WORTH...
A PROPHETIC TRIP?

One day a tax collector came to Peter in Capernaum asking if his teacher paid the temple tax or not. Peter answered him, "Yes." Afterwards, Jesus told Peter to go cast a hook in the sea, take the first fish and open its mouth. In it he would find a piece of money to pay the tax for the two of them (Matthew 17:24-27).

I wonder what Peter thought when Jesus gave him this task? Did he meet anyone on his way to the Sea of Galilee? If so, did they ask him what he was doing? And what would his response have been?

Sometimes the Lord gives me assignments that I do not fully understand but as I obey, and as I go, He gives the understanding. There are times I cannot even explain to others what I am to do.

How do you explain that you are going to build a highway which can't be seen for Jewish people to walk on? That was the assignment the Lord gave us. No bulldozers. No road graders.

These assignments were not tasks accomplished overnight. Some trips took two and a half to three years of prayer and preparation. Through reading God's Word and waiting upon Him, God gave us the plan.

"The battle is the Lord's and He is the Commander in Chief" (2 Chronicles 20:15b; 1 Samuel 17:47).

Matt McLallin, Phillip Israelson, and I had flown from Niigata, Japan, to Khabarovsk, Far East Russia. We were going to build the highway. The highway God had shown me in the August 1974 vision. The vision of the Soviet Jews' release and their return to Israel. Johannes Facius would join us later in Moscow. The Four Smithskis.

We found the ancient gates to the city of Khabarovsk and after praying there, we went to the Amur River to pray there as well. The river is also a gate to this city. It becomes part of the border with China, a short distance away.

Not fully understanding what we were doing, we were obedient to pray as the Lord directed us. When we came to the city of Irkutsk in Siberia, we went to find the gates of the city. Irkutsk is a major terminal on the TransSiberian Railroad located very close to Lake Baikal, one of the largest fresh water lakes in the world. It is a very important transportation city in Russia, and the inland capital of Siberia.

Novosibirsk, our next stop, is the western capital of Siberia.

We went to Lake Baikal after we had been to the gates of the city of Irkutsk. Then we stopped in a small village where we were allowed to get out of our taxi and walk around. However, we didn't meet or see anybody in this little community. It was very, very, very poor. Later we learned there was a prison camp located close by, and the people here were family members of the prisoners. It was a very hard thing to see.

When we returned to our hotel rooms in Irkutsk, Phil came into my room and sat on a chair.

He said, "Steve, I am not going any further on this trip. I refuse to go any further until I understand what we are doing. What kind of prayer is this?"

He had never been involved with any kind of prayer quite like this before. It was rather new to me also, and we were just amazed. However, we were on an assignment from the Lord. When He gave us that assignment we knew we had to carry it out.

Yet Phil still said, "Look, I know the Lord said we are supposed to be here, but I still don't understand anything about the things we are doing. We can't see anything, we don't know what's going on. I have to understand this."

I said, "Phil, do you realize that you are in Siberia, and you're saying you are not going any further?"

He answered, "Not until I understand."

I replied, "I don't know if I fully understand, but I do know this, there is an unseen battle raging in the heavenlies concerning the release of Jews from the Soviet Union, and their return to Israel. We have been commanded by the Lord to come to the gates of the cities to pray. Then, when the time comes for the Jewish people to go, they will be released. There will not be any demonic powers that can hold them back. Somehow, just by our physical presence of coming here and cooperating with God, the release will happen. Because He is fighting the battle in the heavenlies, that's about all I can tell you. We do not wrestle against flesh and blood. The Communists certainly aren't the ones really keeping all the Jewish people here. They are only the instruments being used. It is absolutely the principalities and powers in the unseen realm that are keeping the Jews here."

I was reminded of the Book of Daniel in chapter 10, when after Daniel had been praying for three weeks, an angel came, touched him on his shoulder and spoke to him. The angel told Daniel that he was there to help him understand what was going to happen to the Jewish people. Daniel 10:14 says, "Now I have come to make you understand what will happen to your people in the latter days, for the vision refers to many days yet to come."

However, he had been hindered from coming to Daniel by the Prince of the Kingdom of Persia for twenty-one days. Michael, the archangel, had to come and help the angel, so that he could bring the understanding to Daniel. So I shared with Phil that we were being obedient to God, and as we obeyed, the Lord would do the work and give us understanding. Phil just sat there with a very puzzled look on his face.

I walked over to the window, looked out and said,

"Lord, I am not able to explain anything to Phil. You will have to be the one to reveal it. You have to be the one to show him. Lord, can you do something to reveal the purpose, the plan, the spiritual battle that is going on because of what we are doing?"

Suddenly Phil exclaimed, "My word!"

"What's going on, what's the matter?" I asked.

Phil replied, "Come and sit in this chair, Steve."

So I sat in the chair and Phil said, "Now look at that picture on the wall." Then he said, " Now I understand. Everything is okay."

I looked at the picture on the wall of my room, deep in Siberia in a Communist hotel. This picture had been placed there as a decoration. I know God put this picture there to encourage and explain our assignment to us. It shows a man by his little house with smoke coming out of the chimney. He is tending his cows and there is a large body of water beside the house. Thick clouds are overhead. In the clouds the artist sketched in many things that show that there is a battle going on in the heavenlies. There are dragons, with angels attacking the dragons. There is a man driving four horses into a battle against another dragon. An angel has balls of fire in its hands. Another angel has arrows that are being hurled down against what look like demons. This was all done with the artist's sketching in the clouds. It was a very, very opportune time for that picture to be there because it cleared up everything for us.

Sometimes we are like the man tending the farm animals. We do not know what is going on around us, but there is a huge battle going on in the heavenlies.

Phil said, "This thing is spiritual! Okay, now I can go on. All we have to do is obey God and the Lord will have the angels there. He will fight the battle and we will see the victory."

A reproduction of an ink sketch from a hotel room in the Soviet Union.

I said, "That's right!"

Phil said, "I'm this guy down here tending the sheep! I did not know what was going on; there is a huge battle taking place in the heavenlies."

I was two days in that room and I had not even noticed the picture before. I thought it amazing that the man who did this drawing knew something about spiritual warfare and the battle going on in the heavenlies. The Apostle Paul writes in 2 Corinthians 4:18, ". . . while we do not look at the things which are seen, but at the things which are not seen. For the things which are seen are temporary, but the things which are not seen are eternal."

We have the choice of working in these different realms. Our works in the seen realm are temporary, and are all going to pass away. However, if we work in the unseen realm, the realm of the Spirit, these things will be eternal. From that moment on in Irkutsk, we all understood much better the battle we were in. We also knew we could continue with confidence because the Lord was fighting this battle for us.

CHAPTER 5
GORBACHEV'S OFFICE PRAYER PARTY

"Pray at the office of Mikhail Gorbachev." That was one of the assignments.

Once you have been in that intimate place with the Lord and He gives you a prophetic assignment, there is nothing else to do. You come to a place of trust in the Lord and He begins to change you and trust you. I remember one time the Lord said to share the vision of the release of the Jews from the Soviet Union publicly—in 1974 in the city of Braunschweig. Then God said, "I'm putting a seal on your mouth, you will not share this publicly again until I tell you."

My wife says the greatest miracle of the entire Old Testament was when 600,000 Jewish men, at the commandment of Joshua, marched thirteen times around the walls of Jericho. During this time they could not say one single word. Absolutely nothing. This was a bigger miracle to her than that of the walls coming down.

For six years God said, "Be quiet about what I shared with you." I learned one thing, obedience. So, for six years I was sitting on this vision. You have to understand my nature—I like to talk. However, the Bible says, "A fool tells all . . ." (Proverbs 29:11a). God began to deal with me about keeping my mouth shut. As a result of being quiet and staying silent, a second principle began to happen. God confirmed what He had told me.

He will confirm it in the mouths of two or three witnesses (2 Corinthians 13:1). God will bring people to you who have never heard of you or known anything of what the Lord has spoken to you, because you kept your mouth shut. When you set a guard upon your mouth and the power is not let out, other people will confirm what God has told you.

As a child, I was raised in a railroad town and we had steam locomotives. We are like those giant steam locomotives. I see myself as a huge steam locomotive at the railroad station, ready to go. The engineer pulls the whistle cord to let everybody know the train is going to move, those wheels are going to begin to turn. But if the engineer sits there pulling the cord long enough, all the power goes out the whistle. Guess what your tongue is? It is the whistle. I began to see that, so I closed my mouth. Otherwise, I was letting all the power out. When God would tell me something, if I blabbed it to someone else, it would never come to pass.

When it didn't come to pass, God told me it was because I went and blabbed my mouth. He said I released Him from doing anything because I tried to do it myself. So, I kept my mouth shut. I could not bring 2.7 million Jews out of the Soviet Union. Although, the KGB thought I would!

A KGB agent got saved in a meeting in Finland where I was speaking. At the end of the meeting, she came up to the front and said,

"You have the best kept secret in the whole world."

I asked, "How's that?"

She said, "Because your picture has been given to 600,000 KGB agents. We are trying to find your air force, your bank accounts, your computers, and all of the people who work for you. We are trying to find your organization, and we cannot find anything."

I replied, "Well, the reason is this, I don't even have a secretary, what are you going to find? Because I don't work in the seen realm, I work in the unseen realm."

The KGB did not understand that, so 600,000 KGB agents were chasing Dippy Duck.

She then went on to tell us that spies were being sent to every meeting of ours throughout Scandinavia. She related that they knew who many of my friends were, where I traveled, and other details. I knew she was serious when she told me the full names of my children, my unlisted and unpublished telephone number. They knew about many people in Europe making preparations to help the Soviet Jews, but could find no organization.

She said the KGB was expecting something similar to Israel's raid on Entebe, Uganda. There, the Israelis rescued the Jews from a hijacked Air France airplane. Israel swooped right in under dictator Idi Amin's nose, and took away 206 Jews.

Because everything seemed so secret, they thought I was going to raid the Soviet Union, pick up 2.7 million Jews from a country with eleven time zones, then take them to Israel.

Proverbs 21:3 says, "To do justice and judgment is more acceptable to the Lord than sacrifice." God is looking for a people who will come to understand what He is doing with judgment. "For when Your judgments are in the earth, the inhabitants of the world will learn righteousness" (Isaiah 26:9b). God brings judgment because of His love and His mercy, the watchman understands this. God is going to let us enter into judgment with Him. We see it prophetically throughout the Bible.

Consider Moses; he cooperated with God during His judgement of Egypt. Elijah prayed and it didn't rain for three and a half years, he prayed again and it did rain. He was a man with like passions as ours. ". . . The effective fervent prayer of a righteous man avails much" (James 5:16). Elijah understood what it was to cooperate with God in judgment. Why? He was a friend of God. He had been in intimate relationship and fellowship with God. God wants to do the same with us.

Psalm 119:121: "I have done judgment and justice: leave me not to mine oppressors" (KJV). God is looking for those who will join with Him in judgment and justice. Isaiah 56:1: "Thus saith the Lord, Keep ye judgment, and do justice: for my salvation is near to come, and my righteousness to be revealed. Blessed is the man that doeth this, and the son of man that layeth hold on it" (KJV). God is bringing us to a place where we begin to understand that through judgment God brings deliverance. Why did He bring the Chaldeans against His people Israel? It was to bring them into a place of deliverance. It was in His mercy that He did that. The words of Jesus in Matthew 24 said there would be wars and rumors of wars, and men's hearts would fail them. It is judgment that is coming on the face of the earth, and God is looking for a people who will understand. So God in His mercy, is looking for watchmen who will come and be coworkers together with Him in prayer. His heart is searching everywhere.

The Lord gave us an assignment to go to the Soviet Union with several things to do there. As a Holy Ghost Commando Team, we first went to Mr. Gorbachev's office, which was about two blocks off Red Square, to pray there—fourteen of us. We marched double file just like a commando unit with a spiritual missile. Our missile would be launched in prayer.

I had been to Mr. Gorbachev's office before, so I knew where it was, but others had not. The sign to launch our missile was for me to take off my hat, although the wind was blowing and it was snowing. We were an army; we were God's weapons of war, His battle axes (Jeremiah 51:20).

I'll never forget what happened. It was wild, because we had to march like a commando unit, but God gave us tremendous joy. I mean, this joy within was from the Holy Spirit. As we were marching, we had big smiles on our faces. We turned the corner. We would launch our missile at the front door leading to Mr. Gorbachev's office.

I had not seen so many police, KGB, and army people before. No Russian person walks down that sidewalk, but there we were. The KGB came running across the street, about forty or forty-five of them. They were stunned as they walked along with us. They didn't know what we were planning to do, but it didn't affect us a bit. When we got right in front to where I could reach out and touch the door, I took off my hat. We turned and spoke to each other with smiles on our faces, speaking into the spiritual realm.

Why did God give us so much joy? Proverbs 21:15 says, "It is joy to the just to do judgment" (KJV). With joy at God's direction, we cooperated with Him to do judgment. This missile we launched was into the principalities and the powers over Mr. Gorbachev's office. Mr. Gorbachev was not the problem; he is flesh and blood. We do not wrestle against flesh and blood (Ephesians 6:12), but against principalities, powers, the rulers of darkness of this world, spiritual wickedness in high places. That is where this missile was going. Our missile was found in 1 Samuel 15:23,28, in the words that Samuel said to Saul. "Because you have rejected the word of the LORD, He also has rejected you from being king. The LORD has torn the kingdom of Israel from you today, and has given it to a neighbor of yours, who is better than you."

When we got to the end of the block, all the KGB and police dropped off. We were like little kindergarten children, and started to skip and to dance and we had the best worship service I had been to in a long time.

Why is Mr. Gorbachev no longer president of Russia? Because in January 1986, at God's direction, a Holy Ghost Commando Team went in front of his office and prayed he would be removed.

Another thing we did was pray about the Soviet Union's dealings with weather patterns in different parts of the world. The Soviet Union claimed they could, through psychic powers and electronic equipment, change the weather patterns on any spot on the face of the earth. They claimed they could control nature and acts of God.

During what we called "Operation Clean Sweep", we went to the Lenin Hills overlooking Moscow. "Therefore behold, I am bringing calamity on the house of Jeroboam, and will cut off from Jeroboam every male person, both bond and free in Israel, and I will make a clean sweep of the house of Jeroboam, as one sweeps away the dung" (1 Kings 14:10, NASB).

When we arrived at a viewpoint overlooking the city, an elderly lady was sweeping the area with a home-made broom. We prayed that the occult practices of the USSR to manipulate weather patterns would stop immediately. We then renamed the hills the "Lemon Hills," so that Lenin's name would be removed.

At the end of this assignment our airplane was the last to fly out of Moscow. For five days a very dense fog covered a large area surrounding Moscow and stopped even the trains from running. It was the most dense fog recorded in the past 107 years. All transportation including cars and trucks came to a halt. God confirmed His word.

Other, even more extreme, weather judgments also happened in the Soviet Union, such as reported in *Newsweek*.

"The fishing village of Muinak, once an island, now huddles in the middle of a bleak desert. The dying Aral Sea, . . . laps at gray sand 25 miles away.

"Once the world's sixth largest sea, the Aral has lost two thirds of its volume already, and the water level is dropping nearly a yard per year.

"Even the weather seems to be decaying. A healthy Aral Sea once kept summer temperatures in Muinak in the 90s. Without its moderating effect, the thermometer now leaps as high as 116 degrees fahrenheit."[1]

The Aral Sea lies at the base of the Ural mountains in Russia.

He will not only confirm His word in the mouths of two or three witnesses, He will confirm your assignment with the Word of God, the Bible. You will find scriptures. There hasn't been a time when God has sent us an assignment without giving scriptural backup. He will also give scriptures to more than one person. Why? Amos 3:7, "Surely the Lord does nothing, unless He reveals His secret unto His servants the prophets." He will reveal what He is going to do to more than one person.

We went to the Soviet Union to pray and to cry. I'm not talking about tears streaming down your face, although that certainly happens. But I'm talking about coming to a place where we cry out, "Lord, what is on Your heart. What is my responsibility with that, and what do You want me to do? I ask You to energize me by Your Holy Spirit to be able to cry that out, to bring that forth so that You will come and deliver those who are in bondage" (Exodus 2:23-25). It is our opportunity to stand in the gap for other people. I've seen the burden on the heart of the Lord for 2.7 million Jews in the USSR. Things that happened in the first chapters of the Book of Exodus in the Bible were similarly happening to the Jewish people in the former Soviet Union.

As the pressures got tighter and tighter upon the Soviet Jews, God was looking for a people who would understand what was going on. He was looking for those who cried out with those people who were under bondage, so that God could come and bring deliverance.

There were fifteen of us on this Holy Ghost Commando Team in Moscow. God armed us with some spiritual hand grenades and some spiritual missiles from His Word. The Lord directed us to go and engage in some spiritual warfare at Red Square in a way that I had never done before. We took our weapons and went to Red Square. After forming a circle, we began to enter into the battle, into the war that God wanted us to be a part of. We cried out, along with the Soviet Jews who were under persecution, to stand in the gap so the cry would come up to God. When God hears the cry, He is going to bring deliverance.

As we were standing there, we brought out our first weapon. It didn't look like much. What can you fight with a piece of bread? Yet, 2 Corinthians 10:4 tells us, "For the weapons of our warfare are not carnal but mighty in God for pulling down strongholds." A dear brother, Kjell Sjöberg, a very tall Swede, took out a piece of bread. It doesn't seem like much of a weapon, does it? However, right in Red Square, at one of the corners of the Kremlin, he broke the bread. Something ripped right through the principalities and the powers and the rulers of darkness of this world, and the spiritual wickedness that is over the Kremlin. Right there in Red Square on the Devil's territory, when that bread was broken it signified the body of Christ that was broken. Of Jesus Himself being broken.

Something happened! It was one of the most powerful experiences I've ever had in my walk with God. I can't tell you how I know this. All I can tell you is, I know it. I didn't see it, I didn't hear it, and yet in my spirit I knew it. God from His throne shouted down. He called every demon over Red Square and the Kremlin to attention to see what was happening on their territory in Red Square.

Fifteen men were breaking and eating the body of Christ. We took Holy Communion right there. Remember what Paul said in 1 Corinthians 11:26, "For as often as you eat this bread and drink this cup, you proclaim the Lord's death till He comes." Who are we showing the Lord's death to? To whom do we proclaim that we are taking the body and the blood of Jesus? We are showing it to the principalities and the powers and saying, "Look! You didn't win, Jesus won!" Every time we do that, it wrenches the kingdom of darkness. Jesus' body was broken for us. It says in Ephesians 3:10, that now the church is to show the wisdom of God to the principalities and the powers. The powers of darkness begin to shake and tremble when God empowers us.

When the cry comes up to Him, He comes and delivers us and moves the dark powers back.

It was on New Year's Eve that we were doing this in Red Square. Then Kjell brought out a bottle of wine and opened his coat and started to pour it inside his coat. It was very cold, the snow was coming down and the wind was blowing. We all wondered what he was doing. Then he brought out the next secret weapon. A silver cup, a chalice. This cup happened to be given to him by a Messianic Jewish person who bought it in Israel. When he lifted this up, drunk Russians were coming by. Moscow has the biggest Vodka party of the year on New Year's Eve. They thought we were having a party. They shouted out to us in Russian, "Happy New Year!" We raised the cup and prayed for the release of the Soviet Jews, and sent a cry up to the Lord. We also prayed for a release of evangelism to sweep across the entire Soviet Union, changing that nation. God is looking for a people who understand the cry.

People would ask me, "When is the exodus of the Soviet Jews going to happen?"

My reply was, "When the cry gets loud enough, that is what God is waiting for."

The principle is the same for us. When is deliverance going to come? It will come when the cry becomes loud enough. What is the answer to abortion? Abortion is a stigma that is against the nations. Over 35 million babies have been aborted in the United States alone. You talk about something that is a burden on the heart of the Lord. He is looking for a people who understand what the principle is and will cry out! Why? Because God will answer the cry. What is the answer? The answer is that God is raising a body of believers who know how to intercede and cry out. When God hears that cry, He will come and He will deliver.

Operation Exodus II

CHAPTER 6
LENIN ENTOMBED

During the times I have been at Red Square, on the edge of the Kremlin in Moscow, I have stood and prayed. Once, while standing with my back toward the department store, *Gummi*, God opened my spiritual eyes concerning the tomb of Lenin. God showed me Lenin's tomb being swallowed up by the earth, and the people so frustrated they didn't know what to do. It was as though their god had died. I looked forward to that day so they could receive the true God.

As we were preparing for the Holy Ghost Commando Team to enter the Soviet Union in 1986, the Lord made it clear that we were to pray at Lenin's Tomb. The Russians called it a "holy place", even though they say they don't believe in God.

Whenever Lenin's Tomb was open to the public, thousands of people lined up in a queue that would serpentine through Red Square and at times around the Kremlin walls. Many people came, waiting for a few seconds' glimpse of the decaying body of Lenin still lying in state. The changing of the guard at Lenin's Tomb was also observed by many people.

I never had the desire to go inside Lenin's Tomb to pray on my other journeys to Red Square. However, this time I was ready to do so after the Lord prepared us as a team.

As the Russian people went through the tomb, it seemed like a ritual for them. They would stand very still and reverently, and as they approached the tomb they removed their hats. Psalm 115:4-8 tells about idols and what happens to those who trust in them. Verse 8 says, "Those who make them are like them; so is everyone who trusts in them." You become like what you worship. Lenin is dead; his eyes, mouth, ears, nose, hands, feet, and throat do not function. He is dead, and because you become like what you worship, if you worship Lenin you become spiritually dead. The spirit of death hovered everywhere in the former Soviet Union. Even the flowers didn't have much color. The people looked like zombies. They rarely laughed in public, they didn't seem happy and didn't show much life.

My father owned a funeral home and an ambulance service. I was raised around death from my birth. Therefore, I knew the spirit of death. Consequently, standing in line at Lenin's Tomb gave me an opportunity to deal a blow to the spirit of death entering so many people passing Lenin's remains. This included many young school age children.

Isaiah 65:3-4 says, "A people who provoke Me to anger continually to My face; who sacrifice in gardens, and burn incense on altars of brick; who sit among the graves, and spend the night in the tombs . . ." This is an abomination to God and He says He will repay this (verse 6).

In light of God's Word, I am even more amazed and appalled at people who have the Bible and ignore it by doing these same things. Orthodox Jews go to the graves of dead rabbis surrounded by gardens to pray to them for help. They then leave a small stone on those graves. Sometimes they light candles to them. I have even seen them throw themselves prostrate on a rabbi's grave, crying out to him for help. This should not be so.

Likewise, I have seen people who claim to be Christians do similar things. Some also burn candles and incense on altars and pray to the dead. The Bible makes it very clear that this provokes God to anger; when they do these things, they are no longer putting their trust in Him. God says He will repay them with judgment.

These are occult practices that separate people from God, preventing them from having intimacy with Jesus.

On that New Year's Day we joined the thousands waiting in line to enter Lenin's Tomb. However, we were a Commando Team prepared to do battle.

In the line were many children. Most were from regions throughout the USSR brought there to pay homage to the Father of the Communist Revolution. Instead, the spirit of death was waiting for them, to enter them if possible. The children had already been prepared for this in their outlying cities.

In every Russian city where I had been (over 90 cities) before the breakup of the Soviet Union, I was taken to graveyards where children were the honor guards. They wore uniforms and carried rifles, even very young children. They had a changing of the guard just like the one at Lenin's Tomb. With all this practice at graveyards, containing places dedicated to Lenin in their home cities, they were ready for the occult powers of darkness in Lenin's Tomb itself. One of the most lamentable things I saw in the Soviet Union was this atheistic monster, run by adults, forcing their children to go into this tomb. It is no wonder the Soviet Union collapsed. It was dead and decay had set in.

God help us to raise our children and grandchildren according to His Word, the Bible. God's Word brings life. "My son, give attention to my words; incline your ear to my sayings. Do not let them depart from your eyes; keep them in the midst of your heart; For they are life to those who find them, and health to all their flesh. Keep your heart with all diligence, for out of it spring the issues of life" (Proverbs 4:20-23).

As the fifteen of us came to the entrance of Lenin's Tomb, two Russian soldiers stood on either side of the door. Others were walking up and down the line of people, telling them to be quiet, stand at attention, and take off their hats. It was very cold and snowy and all of us were bundled up. As I entered the tomb, I heard shouting right behind me and turned to see two soldiers' billy-clubs about to strike the heads of two team members. Rauno Kokkola and Pertti Jarvinen from Finland refused to take off their hats. Russia and Finland have an 800-mile common border, and Russia had acted like Goliath. These two "Davids" were not about to pay any respect to Lenin by removing their hats. Instead, the two billy-clubs did. The soldiers did not hit their heads, but knocked off their hats.

Each of us was prepared with our spiritual hand grenades to be thrown in prayer. We were told to continue moving around the three-sided glass cage containing Lenin's remains, and not to say anything. However, we prayed that somehow the Lord would change that. As I went past several soldiers standing inside the tomb and moved around the glass cage, the other team members closed in around the cage. Just then, there was a great disturbance and all the guards inside the tomb ran out, blocking the line so others could not enter. Now, only our team was in Lenin's Tomb. Thus, instead of throwing several spiritual hand grenades, we could pray together as a team, dropping one "bomb" in prayer.

Our prayer bomb was based upon the words of Jesus in the Bible. "Jesus said, 'I am the resurrection and the life.' In the name of Jesus we crush you spirit of death. No man ever again shall eat fruit of you" (John 11:25; Romans 16:20; Mark 11:14). The spiritual realm was penetrated and we knew Jesus gave us the victory again. The guards reentered the tomb and we left. Behind Lenin's Tomb are the graves of other former Soviet leaders. We found Leonid Brezhnev's grave and such joy swept over Kjell Sjöberg, he began to dance upon it.

Since 1991, many statues of Lenin have been removed throughout the former Soviet Union. Even the closing of Lenin's Tomb and the burial of his remains is now more openly spoken of in Russia. Additionally, hundreds of thousands of Jewish people have gone to Israel. God's plan is coming to pass.

"Awake, awake, put on strength, O arm of the LORD! Awake as in the ancient days, in the generations of old. Are You not the arm that cut Rahab apart, and wounded the serpent? Are You not the One who dried up the sea, the waters of the great deep; that made the depths of the sea a road for the redeemed to cross over? So the ransomed of the LORD shall return, and come to Zion with singing, with everlasting joy on their heads; they shall obtain joy and gladness, and sorrow and sighing shall flee away" (Isaiah 51:9-11).

CHAPTER 7
TO RUSSIA WITH GOD

❖

During the afternoon of December 31, 1985, our prayer warfare team entered the walls of the Kremlin. The Lord gave us an assignment to pray at the spot where ceremonies were held for new ambassadors. This was a special place where ambassadors presented their credentials and papers to the Soviet leader.

Since we were ambassadors for the King of Kings (2 Corinthians 5:20), we went to that spot to present our papers. The Lord had given us two papers to deliver.

The fifteen of us were standing against a building on the edge of that place. The cold wind was blowing and the snow was falling. While standing there, I was reminded by the Holy Spirit of my trip to Pittsburgh, Pennsylvania, in May 1984. I was a guest on a television program hosted by Russ and Norma Bixler at WCTV, Wall, Pennsylvania.

The Bixlers had been very dear supporters of Judy and me. After sharing the vision God gave me concerning the Soviet Jews' return to Israel, Russ asked me a very specific question.

He said, "Steve, you said God will judge the idols of the Soviet Union, just as He judged the idols Egypt worshiped at the time of Moses and Pharaoh. Tell us one concrete judgment that will take place so we can know this exodus of Soviet Jews will happen."

In the vision I had in 1974, the first plague the Lord showed me was the judgment of the worship of the idol of Scientific Knowledge in the USSR. The judgment was in the form of a nuclear disaster. For the first time, I was asked to disclose the first judgment. The Lord gave me liberty and this is what I shared on the live TV program.

"When nuclear disasters begin to occur in the Soviet Union, then you will know God has begun to judge the idols of the Soviet Union, and the exodus will certainly happen."

Russ and Norma thanked me for coming and said,

"We will wait to see what takes place."

As our team stood together like a tour group in the Kremlin that day, I pretended to be the guide, holding a map in my hand. If the KGB, a police officer or others passing by looked at us, I simply pointed with my finger and spoke in tongues. Thus, it would appear to them that I was telling the history of the Kremlin.

It was time to deliver to the "Power of Scientific Knowledge" the two papers that the Lord had given to us.

One paper was found in Jeremiah 51:29: "And the land will tremble and sorrow; for every purpose of the

LORD shall be performed against Babylon (in this case the USSR), to make the land of Babylon a desolation without inhabitant." This was a strong judgment to be praying, but God wanted us to cooperate with Him. God was training us in judgment.

According to 1 Corinthians 6:3, one of the things we will do is judge the angels. The Lord is getting us ready by refining us in fire so He can do what is needed in us in order to trust us in cooperating with Him in judgment. He fully tests us so we don't go off on our own, and bring about judgment that He did not tell us about, e.g., Luke 9:54-55.

The second paper was Revelation 8:10: "Then the third angel sounded: And a great star fell from heaven, burning like a torch, and it fell on a third of the rivers and on the springs of water; and the name of the star is Wormwood; and a third of the waters became worm- wood; and many men died from the water, because it was made bitter."

Rauno Kokkola from Finland pointed out the large red star over the Savior's Gate entrance to the Kremlin. Each gate in the Kremlin has a lighted, rotating red star on top of it. Just outside the Savior's Gate on Red Square is the Church of Intercession. We were on the inside of this gate.

We prayed according to these scriptures and a few months later, on April 26, 1986, a meltdown began of the nuclear reactor at Chernobyl. Many people have died since then from this disaster, and certainly no one can inhabit the land, just as the Bible says.

Mr. Gorbachev and the Soviet government did not tell the world of this terrible tragedy. The Swedish government made it known on April 28, 1986.

Judy and I have been privileged to take offerings to the children's wing of Bellingson Hospital in Petah Tikva, Israel. Here, children from the Chernobyl area who have leukemia are brought and treated. Christians in other nations donated the money for these offerings.

The day we prayed inside the Kremlin, we were standing on the most beautiful square in all of Moscow. On this square inside the Kremlin are seven churches, the largest of which is named Saint Michael's, after the archangel for the Jewish people. The highest point in the Kremlin was not one of the red stars over the gates, nor the red flag with the hammer and sickle on it. Instead, the highest point inside the Kremlin of the Communist Party was the cross of Jesus Christ. The cross sat on top of the bell tower of one of the seven churches. Nothing was exalted above the Lord Jesus Christ. Absolutely nothing!

When I returned to the United States, I received a telephone call from Russ Bixler.

Russ said, "Do you remember what you said two years ago here in our TV studio? When will you be on the East Coast again? We need to have you on the program again."

The arrangements were made and before I got there, a Russian nuclear submarine had problems with its reactor and had to be sunk in the Atlantic Ocean.

God is exactly on course with His plans and timing. He is returning the Jewish people to Israel as a prophetic sign to all peoples. First, to keep the covenant He made with Abraham. Second, to announce the return of Jesus the Messiah. And next, to save a nation in a day and fulfill His plan for the nations. He wants all men to be saved and to come to the knowledge of the truth (1 Timothy 2:4). We are about to see an end-time evangelistic thrust beyond anything that has ever happened. All these things are tied to Israel and the return of the Jewish people to their homeland.

The Lord desires that we understand this so we can participate with Him to see His eternal purposes accomplished. As a Father, He longs for His children to be at His side so they can be deeply involved.

CHAPTER 8
DEVIL DEVASTATING
DEPTH CHARGE

The fifteen members of our team were gathered in a room at the Intourist Hotel just off of Red Square. It was the afternoon of December 31, 1985. The biggest vodka party in the world was about to start. On New Year's Eve the Russians in Moscow forget about everything except the party. Tens of thousands of people come to Moscow just to attend this drunken party. I was about to witness the greatest amount of alcohol consumed at any one place that I had ever seen. This turned out to be a wonderful cover for our assignments. Not even KGB agents would follow us; we would be alone without anyone caring about what we did.

Our arsenal of weapons that lay on the bed didn't look very impressive, at least not in the natural. A belt from one brother, ties from others, a stone, a Bible, a pair of suspenders. Each member contributed something for this particular assignment.

As we prayed and quoted scriptures, the anointing of the Holy Spirit became stronger and stronger.

I underlined each scripture as it was mentioned. Each passage dealt with the return of the Jewish people to Israel out of the "north" country and the judgment of the USSR. At the end of our time in prayer, we bound the stone to the Bible with the hand ties, belt, and suspenders. What a depth charge! We were ready for the assignment.

Proverbs 25:2 says, "It is the glory of God to conceal a matter, but the glory of kings is to search out a matter."

After many months of preparing for this trip, I still had several unanswered questions. The Lord had shown me that the Communist leadership of the USSR was receiving power and that it was devilish. However, this power was being given from a place of hiding. Our assignment was to locate the power base of darkness and expose it by shedding the light of God's Word on it. I knew it had something to do with water; the Lord had made that very clear.

Slowly, the Holy Spirit illuminated scripture after scripture to me. After sharing these with my friend, Russ Bixler, from WCTV, he said, "Steve, you are on the right track, but you don't understand yet. God will reveal more to you. The power of Pharaoh is locked somewhere in the rivers, lakes, or seas. You need to search out the scriptures. God will open them up to you and then you will find the power base of the spirit of Pharaoh giving power to the Kremlin. It is not only locking up the Jewish people in the USSR, but is spreading its darkness over many peoples of the earth. That anti-Christ spirit must be confronted and broken in order for the release of the Jewish people to take place. When this spirit is broken, the Gospel can be preached in the Soviet Union and to the rest of the world's population under its control."

The battle is a spiritual one. Soon, revelation came as I studied about the waters in the Bible and how demonic powers use them to hide in. They can be deep and dark places. Perfect covering.

Acts 3:20-21 tells us Jesus Christ will be received in heaven until the time of restoration of all things which God spoke by the mouth of all His holy prophets since time began.

This means the Lord is looking for people to work together with Him for the return of Jesus. To me, this is the most worthwhile endeavor I could ever be involved in.

Revelation 12 tells about the war that broke out in heaven when Michael and his angels cast out the dragon—called the Devil and Satan—to the earth, along with his fallen angels.

The inhabitants of the earth <u>and the sea</u> are warned, because the Devil has come down to them. He has great wrath, because he knows he only has a short time.

The serpent spewed water out of his mouth like a flood toward the woman he was persecuting. However, the earth opened and swallowed the flood.

In chapter 13, John relates what he saw next: "Then I stood on the sand of the sea. And I saw a beast rising up out of the sea . . ." John goes on to describe the beast.

The serpent was trying to counterfeit God by spewing water out of his mouth like a flood. God uses water as a symbol of the Holy Spirit; the enemy always tries to counterfeit God. Satan is not creative and cannot come up with anything new, so he copies. With this, he tries to destroy or control God's children.

After I understood that John was standing on the sand when he saw the beast rise up out of the sea, I began to realize our Commando Team had to deal with a power near the Kremlin. It was in a deep, dark place and the Pharaoh-like spirit giving power to the Soviet leaders had to be exposed. When this demonic spirit is exposed, it loses its power. Light expels or puts out the darkness. Jesus said He is the light of the world and if you follow Him, you will not walk in darkness (John 8:12).

There are places where demons set up their power bases to launch their attacks, especially to enter and control people. However, the Lord is raising up an army to fight and battle them, to expose and kick them out of their hiding places.

Ezekiel 28 speaks of two different kings—a natural king and a spiritual one—the King of Tyre and Lucifer. In verse 2, he claims to sit in the midst of the seas. However, God raises up ones who defeat them. "They shall throw you down into the Pit, and you shall die the death of the slain in the midst of the seas" (Ezekiel 28:8).

Satan always tries to take what is not his.

"The earth is the LORD'S, and all its fullness, the world and those who dwell therein. For He has founded it upon the seas, and established it upon the waters [literally the rivers]" (Psalm 24:1-2). The seas and floods do not belong to the enemy; they belong to God.

God gave us authority to go to Moscow to displace, to depose those powers, because their dwelling place belonged to the Lord.

"He gathers the waters of the sea together as a heap; He lays up the deep in storehouses" (Psalm 33:7). The Lord can do with the seas what He wants to according to His purposes. They belong to Him.

God set boundaries to the waters. The rivers and seas can only go so far. When the enemy tries to use these deep, dark places for cover, he makes them his stronghold. I was greatly encouraged to find out that God set boundaries and that the enemy could not go beyond them. Psalm 104:6-9 points out that the enemy may not pass over His boundaries and may not return to cover the earth.

Proverbs 8:28-29 shows that God put a limit on the sea. The waters can not go beyond that limit or border.

What is the border? Jeremiah 5:22 explains, "'Do you not fear Me?' says the LORD. 'Will you not tremble at My presence, who have placed the sand as the bound of the sea, by a perpetual decree, that it cannot pass beyond it? And though its waves toss to and fro, yet they cannot prevail; though they roar, yet they cannot pass over it." So the boundary is set by the Lord. No matter what the powers of darkness hiding in the waters try to do to come against the Lord, He sets a boundary. The boundary is the sand.

Revelation 13:1 tells us John was standing upon the sand of the sea when he saw the beast rising up out of the sea. God established a border for the sea and a border for the beast. The beast can only go so far, until it is stopped by the border.

Personally, I enjoy lying on the sand at the beach, where the waves are stopped. While at a beach on the Mediterranean, a revelation that came to me through God was what He told Abraham, "In blessing I will bless you, and in multiplying I will multiply your descendants as the stars of the heaven and as the sand which is on the seashore; and your descendants shall possess the gate of their enemies" (Genesis 22:17). The boundary the Lord has set for the enemy is His ancient people, the Jewish people. When the enemy touches the Jews, he is at the same time putting his finger into the pupil of God's eye. "For thus says the LORD of hosts: 'He sent Me after glory, to the nations which plunder you; for he who touches you touches the apple of His eye. For surely I will shake My hand against them, and they shall become spoil for their servants. Then you will know that the LORD of hosts has sent Me'" (Zechariah 2:8-9).

The persecution of the Soviet Jews was the border, and when the Communists touched them, God intervened. He would allow them to go no further.

Satan has tried to annihilate the Jewish people throughout the centuries, because he knows God has a plan for them. However, he cannot succeed, "For I am the LORD, I do not change: therefore you are not consumed, O sons of Jacob" (Malachi 3:6). God has a prophetic purpose for the Jewish people and the enemy cannot stop it.

Psalm 74 relates how God divided the sea and broke the heads of the sea serpents in the waters. He broke the heads of Leviathan and broke open the fountain and the flood, and He dried up mighty rivers. "You have set all the borders of the earth" (Psalm 74:17a). Not only does God establish the borders, He exposes and crushes the enemy from his hiding places. "Have respect to the covenant; for the dark places of the earth are full of the habitations of cruelty" (Psalm 74:20).

Pharaoh in Egypt did not worship the Lord God of Israel. He worshiped many gods. One was the Nile River. In Exodus 7:15, the Lord told Moses to meet Pharaoh at the river's bank. The meeting ended with Moses striking the river and turning it into blood. God judged what Pharaoh was worshiping. Pharaoh was strengthened by the powers of darkness lurking in the Nile. He even had his magicians call upon their demonic powers to do the same. Ezekiel 29 tells of the river worship in Egypt; the Nile represented the powers the Egyptians wanted. It ends up being Devil worship. Each plague was God's judgment on the Egyptians because they worshiped false gods. The Lord chose ten representative idols from the many the Egyptians worshiped, and judged them with plagues.

Satan demands worship, and to get it he hides himself, or disguises himself, even transforming himself into an angel of light (2 Corinthians 11:14). He will do anything he can to deceive, if possible, even the very elect (Matthew 24:24).

God chose the Red Sea to destroy the enemies of the children of Israel. Because the Egyptians worshiped the powers of darkness contained in the waters, the Lord judged them for that. "You rule the raging of the sea; when its waves rise, You still them. You have broken Rahab in pieces, as one who is slain; You have scattered Your enemies with Your mighty arm" (Psalm 89:9-10). Rahab is a name applied to Egypt. It means to act insolently, to rage, to be fierce, to overcome, to behave self-proudly with strength. It turns out to be an epitaph of Egypt. This is a different Rahab than the woman Rahab in the book of Joshua. The names are the same in English, but not in Hebrew.

For the army of Egypt, God chose the Red Sea in which to destroy it—the very thing they worshiped. Rahab was wiped out. "For it is written, 'He catches the wise in their own craftiness'" (1 Corinthians 3:19; Job 5:13).

Psalm 93:3-4, Proverbs 30:4, and Job 26:10-12 tell us the Lord is mightier than the waves of the sea. "'Or who shut in the sea with doors . . . When I fixed My limit for it, and set bars and doors; when I said, 'This far you may come, but no farther, and here your proud waves must stop'" (Job 38:8,11)! Mark chapter 4 relates the story of when Jesus and His disciples were in a boat on the Sea of Galilee and a big storm came. The enemy was trying to drown the Messiah and His disciples.

I once witnessed a storm on the Sea of Galilee and it was so ferocious, I was afraid just standing on the shore. Waves reaching over twenty feet high have been recorded during storms on the Sea of Galilee.

Jesus stood up and rebuked the winds and said to the sea, "Peace, be still." He forbade the wind and censored it. He silenced the sea; He brought it to an involuntary stillness. Jesus muted it and put a muzzle on it, the very sea itself. He has been given all power in Heaven and in earth, and He wants all true believers in Him to cooperate with Him.

"In that day the LORD with His severe sword, great and strong, will punish Leviathan the fleeing serpent, Leviathan that twisted serpent; and He will slay the reptile that is in the sea" (Isaiah 27:1). Leviathan means a serpent, to twine and unite, to encircle and bind up people. This is what the enemy tries to do. Isaiah says he is in the sea and God will slay him with a sword.

Psalm 89:25 says, "Also I will set his hand over the sea, and his right hand over the rivers." God is giving His power to another whom He can trust, to see His plan become a reality. I decided long ago that I wanted to be a warrior in God's army. I have the nature of my God (2 Peter 1:4) and will tolerate nothing that tries to change that.

One facet of His nature is that He is like a man of war. There are a number of things in the Body of Christ that have slithered in to rob the people from being warriors. I have noticed it in some praise songs and ministries that make Christians focus on themselves. They are designed to make people introspective to the point of becoming selfish, and claiming it's from the Lord. The result being that people go deeper and deeper into themselves, reducing them to spineless sheep unable to answer the end-time call spoken of in Joel 3:9, "Proclaim this among the nations: 'Prepare for war! Wake up the mighty men, let all the men of war draw near, let them come up.'"

"For our God is a consuming fire" (Hebrews 12:29). Not "like" a consuming fire; He IS a consuming fire. "It is a fearful thing to fall into the hands of the living God" (Hebrews 10:31).

"The LORD shall go forth like a mighty man; He shall stir up His zeal like a man of war. He shall cry out, yes, shout aloud; He shall prevail against His enemies" (Isaiah 42:13). "The LORD is a man of war" (Exodus 15:3a).

Our team had the fighting spirit of the Lord and with this foundation in the Word, we were ready to do battle.

The Moscow River winds its way along the western side of the Kremlin, down past Red Square. One of the things the Lord revealed in prayer was that the leadership of the Soviet Union sought power from external spiritual forces. Satan was poised and ready to give them power.

Our assignment was to go and expose those dark spiritual forces giving power to the leaders of the USSR. With that power broken and exposed, they could no longer hold the Jews captive. The forces keeping the country together and stopping mass evangelism had to be pushed back.

Jeremiah 51 was our battle plan. It speaks of the utter destruction of Babylon, and the principles that would be used to destroy the Kremlin and Communism. Every word spoken by the holy prophets of old will come to pass. God is searching for those in His body to work together with Him to see the powers of darkness pushed back at this time.

Jeremiah 51:12-13 says to set up the standard on the walls. The guard had to be strong watchmen, because the LORD was going to carry out His ambushes against those who dwell by many waters. Their end has come and also their covetousness.

We were literally a spiritual guerrilla warfare team sent to ambush the enemy in the Kremlin. As guerrillas, you can do great damage and cause havoc to the enemy.

We set up a 24-hour prayer chain among the fifteen of us and we prayed through Jeremiah 51 many times. We had to be on our spiritual toes with our ears open to hear what the Spirit said. The location of the ambush was also an important factor.

In verse 15, God speaks of creating the earth, the heavens, and the seas; all belonging to God. These areas do not belong to demonic powers.

In Psalm 89:10, we see that God scatters His enemies with His mighty arm. In Isaiah 27:1, we see that He punishes leviathan with His severe, strong sword. Who is the severe, strong sword? The answer is in Jeremiah 51:20: "You are My battle-ax and weapons of war: For with you I will break the nation in pieces; with you I will destroy kingdoms; . . ." Now, telling yourself you are a battle-ax may not be the most edifying thing you have told yourself lately, but it is true. We become the strong sword of the LORD, in His hand.

As we obey Him in carrying out His instructions, He begins to use us as His sword or battle-ax, to slay the dragon, the leviathan in the sea. He is preparing His battle-axes. I love being a battle-ax in the hand of the LORD.

Verse 52 of Jeremiah chapter 51 says, "'Therefore behold, the days are coming,' says the LORD, 'that I will bring judgment on her carved images, and throughout all her land the wounded shall groan.'" As a guerrilla warfare team, in prayer we went against the graven images of the Kremlin, Lenin's Tomb, the office of the Central Committee of the Communist Party, Gorbachev's office, the Ecomocon headquarters for finance, eventually the KGB, and the very foundation of the USSR.

Verses 55-57 continue, "Because the LORD is plundering Babylon (in our case, the Soviet Union) and silencing her loud voice, though her waves roar like great waters, and the noise of their voice is uttered, because the plunderer comes against her, against Babylon, and her mighty men are taken. Every one of their bows is broken; for the LORD is the God of recompense, He will surely repay. And I will make drunk her princes and wise men, her governors, her deputies, and her mighty men."

What has happened to the loud voice of the former Soviet Union? What happened to Mr. Gorbachev, her mighty man? What has happened to the power of the Soviet Union? They have been judged by the LORD God of Israel.

That New Year's Eve, with so many drunk people, the likes of which I have never seen before, reminded me of Jeremiah 51:57. However, the drunkenness would be much deeper than vodka could induce. The princes, wise men, governors, deputies, and mighty men would not be able to sleep off this intoxication.

"So Jeremiah wrote in a book all the evil that would come upon Babylon (for us the USSR), all these words that are written against Babylon. And Jeremiah said to Seraiah, 'When you arrive in Babylon and see it, and read all these words, then you shall say, "O LORD, You have spoken against this place to cut it off, so that none shall remain in it, neither man nor beast, but it shall be desolate forever." Now it shall be, when you have finished reading this book, that you shall tie a stone to it and throw it out into the Euphrates (for us the Moscow River). Then you shall say, 'Thus Babylon shall sink and not rise from the catastrophe that I will bring upon her. And they shall be weary'" (Jeremiah 51:60-64).

What a depth charge!

I submitted this to my brothers to test if it was from the Lord. To a man, they agreed it was.

We had to find a stone, but the ground was covered with snow. God provided it—that is a story in itself. It was quite a large stone, and after we found it the bus driver looked at us rather strangely as we boarded the bus to go back to our hotel.

With our preparations complete, we attended the New Year's Eve Party. The enemy tried to discourage us from our mission when we sat back at the banquet tables earlier that evening. Someone said, "What if the police or KGB stop us or ask what we are doing, and they find the Bible tied to the stone, what do we do?" Fear began to hang around us, looking for an entrance into any one of us.

Satan never has anything new. He deceived Eve with a doubting question, "Has God indeed said . . ." (Genesis 3:1)? He attempted to do the same to Jesus in

Luke 4:3, "If You are the Son of God . . . ?" But Jesus kept Himself obedient by quoting the Word of God. After all, in Luke 3:22, a voice came from heaven that said, "You are My beloved Son." Jesus did not doubt, He believed His Father.

Satan tried this very same tactic with us at the New Year's Eve Party by instilling fear. However, we brought a secret weapon on this trip. One of our team members was a university professor from Sweden. In the large banquet hall, there were booths, each with high sides, so you could not see who was sitting in the next one. I was sitting at the open end of the booth and next to me was a table loaded with vodka, champagne, and mineral water, especially for our table. As I looked around the hall, I could see only those sitting at the ends of their tables with their alcohol beside them.

As that spirit of fear hovered over us, the professor, who was hidden from the view of the other booths, began to laugh. I had never seen anyone laugh with his whole body before; I could not even imitate it, it was like a bomb going off. It was the funniest laugh, and I began to laugh too, almost falling off my chair. Soon the person sitting at ends of the other booths started laughing too, that started their party laughing and it spread through the entire hall. Only we knew why we were laughing. Some of the people came over to see why we laughed and saw that none of the liquor on our table had been touched, so they traded us their mineral water.

The joy of the Lord is our strength. The doubt left and so did we, to carry out our assignment.

After the Russians were good and drunk, we dressed for the severe cold and snow outside. Taking our marked Bible tied to the stone, we made our way across Red Square to a bridge at the edge of the Kremlin that crossed the Moscow River.

As we were gathered there, my friend, Johannes Facius, read Psalm 137. "By the rivers of Babylon, there we sat down, yea, we wept when we remembered Zion. We hung our harps upon the willows in the midst of it. For there those who carried us away captive required of us a song, and those who plundered us required of us mirth, saying, 'Sing us one of the songs of Zion!' How shall we sing the LORD'S song in a foreign land? If I forget you, O Jerusalem, let my right hand forget her skill! If I do not remember you, let my tongue cling to the roof of my mouth — If I do not exalt Jerusalem above my chief joy" (Psalm 137:1-6).

We prayed for the release of the Soviet Jews. As we lifted up the Bible tied to the stone, I looked below and realized why we had found such a large one—the Moscow River was frozen. The big stone would crash through the ice. We then quoted Jeremiah 51:62.

As we cast it into the river we pronounced the words of Jeremiah 51:64, "Soviet Union, you shall sink and never rise again."

This spiritual depth charge was so devastating to the Devil that he lost his strangle hold on the Soviet Union keeping the Jewish people there. A spiritual battle took place in the heavenlies. God sent His angels and the rest is history. God had the victory!

Our team had such a release, we went skipping through Red Square like little children, screaming and shouting. No one paid us any attention because Red Square was full of loud and staggering drunks. However, we were wild with enthusiasm. We were rejoicing in the LORD.

The spiritual climate over the Kremlin was changed.

Somehow the testimony of this incident got around to different people in the Soviet Union. Several people I met during subsequent visits to Russia expressed their concern over a Bible being thrown in the Moscow River during a time when Bibles were so very scarce. They did not understand that it was a prophetic act opening the door for millions of Bibles to be brought into the Soviet Union. As a result, this has now occurred.

Operation Exodus II

CHAPTER 9
LEMON GRENADE

During the beginning of 1986, the Lord began to impress Kjell Sjöberg and me to make another trip into the Soviet Union with a group of prayer warriors. As we sought the Lord concerning what He wanted accomplished on this trip, we also prayed about the timing.

Timing is very important. I believe timing is as important as the assignment itself. I can't stress this strongly enough. I have tried to do things that were not in God's time. Everything fell through because it was not exactly in the timing that the Lord had wanted things to be done. Matthew chapter 3 is a good example of this. God's timing for Joseph was also perfect, "Until the time that his word came to pass, the word of the LORD tested him" (Psalm 105:19).

In April 1987, I was staying in Kjell and Lena Sjöberg's home not far from Stockholm, Sweden.

Kjell informed me, "I know the timing we are to be in Moscow."

I asked, "When?"

He replied, "October 17th, we have to be in Moscow on October 17th because of the October

Revolution." And I thought immediately, Oh, that's right! October 17, 1987, is 70 years after the Bolshevik Revolution in the Soviet Union, October 17, 1917.

So, exactly 70 years! Boy, I got excited. Why did I get excited? Because there was another release of Jewish people after a 70-year captivity. That captivity was the Babylonian captivity. A saying went around in the body of Christ some years ago. "God said it, I believe it, that settles it!" Can I tell you that is not totally true? God said it, I believe it, I prayed it, it happened, then it was settled.

What did Daniel do? In Daniel 9:2, he understood the prophecies of the 70 years of the Babylonian captivity recorded in the book of Jeremiah. Daniel had the prophetic word and he knew what God was going to do. However, when you read verse 3 you find what Daniel did with the prophetic word. He put on sackcloth and ashes and he prayed and fasted until the Jewish people were released from the Babylonian captivity. The first Jewish person didn't return until two years after Daniel's prayer.

I don't know what a long time to you is, but my mother prayed thirty-one and a half years before her immediate family was saved.

I said, "Mom, how could you pray for us that long? Especially when I came home drunk, belligerent or angry, mean or rebellious."

She said, "What are you talking about, son? I saw you preaching the gospel of Jesus all over the whole world. I saw you laying hands on the sick and they were healed. I saw people being filled with the Holy Spirit. What are you talking about, son?"

I replied, "Oh, please excuse me!"

She called those things that were not as though they were (Romans 4:17). Thirty-one and a half years . . . Who cares how long it took after it's done and everyone is in! No microwave prayer, no instant coffee prayer, no convenient Christianity—add water, mix, and you have instant neat. No, thirty-one and a half years of prayer before the last member of the family, my sister, received salvation through faith in Jesus the Messiah.

People have asked me if I ever got discouraged during the years between 1974, when the vision was given, and when the Soviet Jewish people began to go to Israel. I certainly have had discouragements, but not about the exodus of the Soviet Jews. The Lord told me in 1974 I would see them return to Israel during my lifetime. Thus, I was continually inspired to pray.

No one is more blessed than I am that over 900,000 Jewish people from the former Soviet Union are now in Israel. Why they are returning, is just as great to me as that they are returning. I am so appreciative to the Lord, for in His timing He has allowed me to live to see these end-time events.

Timing. Very important. When Kjell said to me October 17th was the 70th anniversary, I said,

"Okay, the problem is that I'm speaking at a convention during that time in October."

He replied, "That's simple, let's just have the Lord cancel it and change it to a later date and you'll be fine."

I said, "That would be a good confirmation."

Two days later I got a call and they had to move the dates for that convention. I was now freed up to go to Moscow and I knew we had the timing.

Twelve men were invited to be part of the team. On this trip, twelve was the number because the Lord impressed us with the twelve judgment thrones in Matthew 19:28. Other trips required different numbers of men.

One of the team members was Jamie Schneider, a young man from Fairbanks, Alaska. Jamie was in his twenties and quite excited to go. The previous year he had been out fishing along the Yukon River in Alaska. While hiking along the eastern bank of the Yukon, he found a piece of driftwood that looked like a rod or staff. He was strongly impressed by the Holy Spirit to take that stick home. However, he wondered whatever he would do with it, so he threw it back onto the river bank.

Jamie had a friend who went fishing the following week, and while walking along on the east bank of the Yukon River he found a stick. He knew nothing about the fact that Jamie had been at that same place the week before. He picked it up and related that the Lord had shown him to take this piece of wood, looking like a staff, to Jamie.

It was exactly the same piece of driftwood Jamie had picked up one week earlier. Jamie put it in his closet for a year and told no one about it. When he was invited to join our "strike force" the Holy Spirit impressed him, "Take that rod with you to the Soviet Union." He felt quite weird, but he obeyed.

His thoughts raced with, "What would the other team members think? Walk around Moscow with a large staff?" It sounded like the Old Testament to him, like Moses going to Pharaoh's court.

Jamie asked the Lord to confirm his bringing the rod according to 2 Corinthians 13:1. Some days later, I sent a letter to all the team members with a list of scriptures to help prepare us before meeting together in Finland. Strategy and assignments would be based on these Bible verses. This helped to tune us into one unit, so when we got together God could melt us into one.

Three of the scriptures had to do with a rod and a staff. Jamie was thankful for the confirmation and put the rod in a large garment bag that he could not fold because of the rod's length.

Jamie and I flew together to Finland.

On the plane Jamie said, "Steve, I brought something with me, but I don't know if I should tell you about it or not."

I replied, "It is better to be quiet about whatever it is and let God confirm it to you."

The first day we were together, Kjell Sjöberg said, "I have just come from Yugoslavia and looked in many places for a staff. I believe we should be like Moses when we go to Moscow and have a rod with us. I even went out in the forest this morning, here in Finland, but I could not find one."

Jamie jumped up to go to his room and Kjell said, "Oh, I probably could not find one because you have it hidden in your suitcase."

We all laughed. Jamie came back with his piece of wood. It was the most awesome looking staff. The head on it looked like it had snakes coming out of it.

All of us went hilarious. What would the customs think? The KGB would have no problem locating us. We certainly wouldn't be trying to hide or disguise ourselves. It was simply a symbol. Every time we prayed we were to stomp the staff to seal our prayers. Satan cannot seal; he can mark, but he cannot seal. Only ambassadors for Jesus Christ can seal! And when that prayer is sealed, the enemy cannot break it, it is done, that's it! Satan's movements are in the open and cannot be sealed. That is why he uses deception. Nehemiah 6:5 tells us Sanballat sent his servant five times with an open letter to Nehemiah. Sanballat wanted to stop the work of God, but he could not seal the matter.

However, Nehemiah and his representatives did seal their matters. "'And because of all this, we make a sure covenant, and write it; and our leaders and our Levites and our priests seal it.' Now those who placed their seal on the document were:" (Nehemiah 9:38,10:1). Then follows a long list of those who sealed the document.

Sometimes our prayers are not answered because we did not seal them in God. But when we do seal a matter, it prevents the enemy from stealing it.

Why use this particular piece of wood? It represented a boundary stopping Russia. Alaska once belonged to Russia. The Russians penetrated into Alaska only as far as the Yukon River. The native Indians were too fierce and did not let the Russians cross the Yukon River; it was a boundary and the Russians could go no further. In 1867, William Henry Seward purchased Alaska from Russia for $7,200,000. It was known at that time as Seward's Icebox, or Seward's Folly. Jamie's rod was laying on the east bank of the Yukon River and represented a barrier so that the Russians could go no further. We would be praying the Russians could go no further with the Soviet Jews, they met their barrier in God and He would now say, "Give them up!" (Isaiah 43:6).

This same morning I jokingly said to my brothers,

"You know, it's going to be the Feast of Tabernacles when we go into Russia. I wonder if we shouldn't find some etrogs. (An etrog is a citron, a special kind of lemon. During the Feast of Tabernacles it is one of the things that every Jewish man takes into the synagogue. It is a symbol of the fruit from the harvest.) Possibly, in Moscow we may go to the synagogue and they might not have their etrogs. I don't know if we can get them here in Finland, but maybe we should take some with us."

We continued in our prayers and plans for the strike we were going to make on that assignment. The next morning, my brothers said, "We believe that we are supposed to take those lemons. That was prophetic and that was from God."

I said, "You do? Well, I don't think there's any possibility at this late date in finding the etrogs, but maybe we can find some lemons, and we'll just have to use them as substitutes."

On our way to the airport, we stopped at a store to find some lemons. When I went in, I found the largest lemons I have ever seen. They were almost the size of small grapefruits. They were huge. I started laughing as I bought one for each man on the team; I gave one to each of them when we arrived at the airport. I shoved mine into my overcoat; I could barely get it into the big pocket. We must have been some sight. Walking around with a large staff, lemons in our pockets, going into a battle that can't be seen with the natural eye.

So we flew into Moscow and after the plane landed, all of my brothers passed through customs very quickly. On other trips I have passed through, or I have been watched and searched. However, this time the custom officials held me up and didn't return my passport. When my luggage arrived, a uniformed man came to me, told me to grab my suitcase and showed me into a back room. In the room there was a long table, and he said to put my suitcase on it and open it. I thought of all the trips I had made to the Soviet Union and how they had tried to intimidate me before. So I thought, Lord, I don't know what is going on, but I need to be released from here to get back to the rest of my brothers so we can go on the assignments that You gave us.

A very, very stern looking officer then came in. I thought somehow I had to get these men to laugh, and I didn't know how. So I just said, "Lord, help me." They went through everything in my suitcase, every piece of clothing. They were checking every button on every shirt. So I took a shirt up to them and said,

"Oh, would you like to speak into my button, please?"

Well, they didn't think that was funny at all, although I felt it was quite clever. I thought, well, that didn't work. They pushed me aside and began to squeeze my toothpaste to make sure I hadn't opened the end and stuffed something inside. They were sticking needles into the soles of my shoes to make sure they were not hollow. They went through everything very, very carefully. They checked my suitcase very thoroughly to see that there were no hidden compartments of any kind. Then they said,

"Okay, now we're going to do a strip search. Begin by emptying all of your pockets here on this end of the table."

I reached my hand into my pocket and then remembered I had this great big huge lemon there. Now, in all the times I've been in the Soviet Union there are certain things I had never seen there. I had never seen an orange; I had never seen a banana; I had never seen lemons. These were things that you just didn't see in the Soviet Union. They don't grow them there. My hand was on this lemon and I thought, Lord, you turned water to wine, I'm asking that you would turn this lemon into a hand grenade if you have to. When I pull it out I'm going to say something, and I believe in faith,

Jesus, that you are going to give me the words that will get me released so I can go back to my other team members. So I pulled out this big lemon and rolled it slowly across the table. It went bloop, bloop-bloop, bloop. They stared at this thing and then looked at me. I opened my mouth and in faith began to speak.

"I know why you are doing this to me."

The officer looked at me and shouted, "You do? Why?"

I replied, "It's for my safety!"

And the officer said, "For your what?"

And he started to laugh, because he couldn't believe I had said, "For my safety."

See, when you fly in and out of Israel you go through a very, very thorough security check because they are looking for anybody who would try to sneak something onto a plane to either hijack it or cause an act of terrorism. So the officer began to laugh and the other man began to laugh. Finally the officer said,

"Forget it. Get this man out of here."

They threw my clothes back into the suitcase, I grabbed it, went over to the door and started to go out, when the officer said, "Hey!" I turned back and he threw the lemon to me. I just put it in my pocket and walked out that door.

Again, I found that sometimes it takes the foolish things to confound the wise, as the scripture says (1 Corinthians 1:27). When you have a confirmation that the Lord has told you to do something, no matter how small, no matter how insignificant, or even how easy it may sound, it could very possibly save your life when you act upon it.

And again, I had a lesson in obeying the Lord in even the smallest of things.

CHAPTER 10
GOD'S LITTLE STONIES

A major reason we made this particular trip to the Soviet Union, was that the Lord wanted us to be there on the 70th anniversary of the Bolshevik Revolution. Lenin declared the nation in October of 1917. Seventy years later, we were going to be in the exact same place, which today houses the Bolshoi Theater in Moscow. We went there to cancel the Constitution of the USSR.

Just before we left to go out to do that particular assignment, we were in our hotel when Kjell Sjöberg got a deep impression to record what we were going to do for posterity. So we checked among ourselves, and not one of us had brought a tape recorder.

We decided we would look for a tape recorder on the way to where Lenin had signed the Constitution. Trying to find anything in Moscow was very difficult. However, as we were walking on our way, we saw a fountain that had a stone in it. This stone was about the size of a Sony or a Panasonic tape recorder. So we thought it would be perfect; we would use that as our tape recorder.

So here we go. We have a staff and the youngest man is carrying it. We felt that the youngest man should use it rather than the oldest, to confound the wise.

We have our lemons in our pockets, and now we have this stone. And off we go to cancel the Constitution of the Soviet Union in prayer.

As we approached the place that is now the Bolshoi Theater, four KGB agents picked us up and walked along with us. Recognizing the KGB agents this time was easy because they all dressed exactly alike—leather coats and the exact same hats—they were very easy to pick out. They followed us as we made our circle at the theater.

It must have been quite an amazing thing to see, and again I wondered what these KGB agents reported back to their headquarters. Here we were with a young man holding a wooden staff, with lemons in our pockets, and talking into a stone, passing it around the circle.

In Joshua 24:26-27 it says: "Then Joshua wrote these words in the Book of the Law of God. And he took a large stone, and set it up there under the oak that was by the sanctuary of the LORD. And Joshua said to all the people, "Behold, this stone shall be a witness to us, for it has heard all the words of the LORD which He spoke to us. It shall therefore be a witness to you, lest you deny your God."

Before the first Sony or Panasonic, God came out with the first tape recorder. Jesus spoke in Luke 19:40, "I tell you that if these should keep silent, the stones would immediately cry out." Now how could the stones cry out unless they had recorded the worship and the praises of Heaven since the beginning of creation?

So God has His little "stonies" that He can turn on which have the witness and testimony of what He has done through the ages.

CHAPTER 11
USSR's CONSTITUTIONAL CONVENTION

With the little "stonie" now in our possession to record the main event of this trip, we proceeded to the very place where Lenin signed the Constitution of the USSR.

It was many months previous when the Lord had spoken to my heart and said to me, "It is enough, it is over. Go to the Soviet Union and cancel its Constitution so the Soviet Jewish people can go to Israel."

Lenin laid the groundwork for the Soviet Constitution during the Bolshevik Revolution of 1917. Three subsequent constitutions were put forth by the supreme governing body, the All-Russian Central Executive Committee (VtsIK) in 1918, 1924, and 1936. As a result the Supreme Soviet, the Central Committee, and the all powerful Politburo were formed.

The Soviet Constitution should not be considered a democratic constitution. Since the Soviets never gave much credence to their constitution, it was powerless for its citizens. The dictatorship had the power, the secret police, and the armed forces to carry out its wishes. This is why the constitution had to be changed.

Our team was prepared. Each man had prayed and sought God before going on this trip to cancel a portion of the USSR's Constitution. Then in prayer, we would rewrite or make new amendments bringing forth a new constitution.

Again, the seventy-year captivity of the Jewish people was coming to an end. Just as Jeremiah had prophesied, Daniel understood and prayed until they were released from Babylon. This was part of our prayer strategy, so that the Soviet Jews would also be released.

It was seventy years after the October 1917 Revolution, when Lenin signed the constitution, that we walked up to the same building. Atop this building was a chariot with four horses. Zechariah speaks of four horses, and the book of Revelation also speaks of four horses. They went out over the earth and power was given them.

What happened after October 1917? The Bolsheviks changed their name to Communists. The tentacles of Communism began its dominion over 70% of the earth's population. Those horses had gone with power.

However, God said, "It is enough, it is over." The power of Communism would be broken; the Iron Curtain would fall; the Berlin Wall would come down; and a new constitution would be written based on the Bible. Why? Communism had to fall. It was not to be an end-time power. The spirit of Babylon is much stronger and will be an end-time power that God will deal with.

As the twelve of us gathered in a circle, we must have been some sight for the four KGB agents following us. Lemons in our pockets, stomping a wooden staff as each man prayed, and speaking into a stone. They came closer and closer trying to hear us. When I was praying, one agent was so close his elbow was touching my back and his hand was cupped to his ear to hear better. I don't know why he did that, I was praying in the Holy Spirit and I know he couldn't understand that.

We prayed that the Soviet people would have civil liberties, that the Jews would be allowed to immigrate to Israel, and that Christians would be allowed to have open meetings. We used Bible scriptures as the basis. For instance, Isaiah 2:3, ". . . For out of Zion shall go forth the law, and the word of the LORD from Jerusalem." Isaiah 33:22, "For the LORD is our Judge, the LORD is our Lawgiver, the LORD is our King; He will save us." These are some topics we took up in writing the new Constitution.

We had the marvelous presence of the Lord with us. We knew He also sent angels to be there and I believe some of them were big ones. Each time we finished a point in prayer, we stomped the rod to seal the prayer. It was like an "Amen!" Something also happened in heaven and we looked forward to the answers to our prayers.

The answers began to come in 1988 when Mr. Gorbachev changed part of the USSR's Constitution and called for a complete change in 1989. During 1990, unprecedented numbers of Soviet Jews began to go to Israel, and by 1991 the aliyah was in full swing. Millions of Bibles were taken into Russia and great evangelization began.

Prayer is exciting. It has never been dull for me.

As we were returning to our hotel, we were all struck with awe by the presence of the Lord. We came to the fountain from where we had taken the stone. We then placed it back there. To my knowledge, it is still there to this day as a record of what we did.

The Supreme Soviet of the Soviet Union did not change the constitution. God changed that constitution. The Politburo did not change the constitution. God changed the constitution of the Soviet Union and it is recorded in that rock. Just as Joshua had his stone, we had our stone. Maybe God will play it back one day.

After praying at the theater, we went to our next destination, the economic headquarters of the USSR and the Communist Bloc countries.

Two weeks before this trip, Kjell Sjöberg received a phone call from a fellow Swedish friend who was in the Kingdom of Tonga. Tonga is one of the smallest kingdoms in the world. The King of Tonga received Ezekiel 27:25-27 in prayer. What impressed him most was from verse 26, ". . . But the east wind broke you in the midst of the seas." So the king of Tonga prayed a prayer concerning world economy according to Ezekiel.

These people knew we were going to the Soviet Union, and asked if we would continue the king's prayer, since he was as far east as possible. They felt the economy of Israel and the return of the Soviet Jews were also part of this. God was about to shake up the world economy.

Standing in front of the Econocom building, we prayed judgment concerning the finances of the world, especially in the Communist Bloc countries. We prayed in agreement with what was started to the east, from the little Kingdom of Tonga. That was the evening of October 17, 1987.

When we left the Soviet Union and found out about the stock market crash on Monday, October 19, we understood our prayer. God wants to trust His children with being the most informed people on the face of this earth. He gives us opportunity to cooperate with Him. He is the God of history. He desires to let His power and authority be released in His children whom He can trust, to change the course of nations.

The power of God is not for playing games, nor to be treated lightly. However, we do get to participate with the Lord to see his righteousness established on earth. "For as many as are led by the Spirit of God, these are sons of God" (Romans 8:14).

CHAPTER 12
KGB KOLLAPSE

The Lord quickened different scriptures to me concerning praying at the KGB headquarters. Beside each of these verses I wrote "KGB" in my Bible. I did not share any of these with the others. I knew we would pray at the headquarters of the KGB and the Lord was preparing me for that.

Whenever God gives us an assignment, He always backs it up with scriptures and confirms His word through others, as Amos 3:7 says. He will tell more than one person His secret, to confirm that the Lord is directing us. The Lord gives us our strategy for our prayer assignments in His Word. This is vital because we are dealing with principalities, powers, rulers of the darkness of this age, and spiritual hosts of wickedness in the heavenly places according to Ephesians 6:12. This is not a light thing, and we cannot be flippant or presumptuous. Otherwise the enemy strikes back, you find you have removed yourself from God's protection and you are the victim. I tell about such an incident in Chapter 15.

Before this trip, I was looking for people who would confirm what we were about to do. I had no idea who the people would be, so when someone came to me and shared a confirmation, it was such a blessing.

I was speaking in a town in Pennsylvania where I had never been. A lady came up and handed me some scriptures and said, "These don't mean a thing to me, do they mean anything to you? I was prompted by the Lord to give them to you."

I looked at the list and exclaimed, "Do they ever!"

They were the very scriptures the Lord had given me concerning the KGB.

During April 1987, I was a guest again of Kjell and Lena Sjöberg in Sweden. The first morning I came to the breakfast table, sitting beside my plate was a list of scriptures.

I asked, "What is this?"

Kjell answered, "God woke me up in the middle of the night, Steve, and He had me write these scriptures down. As I was reading them, I thought this was the strategy that the Lord wants us to pray at the KGB Headquarters in Moscow on the next trip."

As I looked over the list I got so excited. I handed Kjell my Bible and asked him to look up each scripture. He wondered why, but he opened my Bible, and next to each scripture he saw I had written "KGB". Exactly the scriptures the Lord had given me, He gave to that lady in Pennsylvania and to another on the opposite side of the world. God always confirms the assignment.

The more confirmations you receive, the more difficult the assignment will be. When I am given many confirmations I know I will need them because the battle will be intense. When the battle gets really tough, you can say, "No, Devil, you cannot stop me because of . . ." You can then list all the confirmations; then you will continue in the battle until it is won.

During our trip in October 1987, as we walked through the streets of Moscow at night, we walked with a purpose. We walked in the victory Jesus won for us on the cross.

Kjell was a tall man and had a long stride. I am average height and am always trying to keep up with him. However, that night, it was as if the angels were carrying me and I was out in front. It was the only time Kjell said, "Steve, wait up. You are moving so fast, but I don't see your legs moving."

We had a sense of destiny, a feeling that history would be made that night.

We came to the big square in front of the KGB headquarters. In the midst of this square was a statue of Dzerzinsky, the founder of the KGB. Underneath the KGB building was the Ljublanka prison, the most notorious prison in all the USSR. The fear of the Soviet people was, if you were seen taken in by the KGB, you would never be seen again. From the sides of this square were entrances to the Metro.

We approached the Metro subway tunnel that went under the street. The tunnel also went under part of the headquarters itself.

When we were just inside the tunnel, a drunken man fell down a number of steps, hit his head and was bleeding. Two or three men on our team started toward the man to help him; Kjell rebuked them and told them to rejoin the team immediately. They were well disciplined and knew better than to ask why. They simply obeyed. When you are a leader of a commando team and the enemy is right there, you give the commands and there is no time to answer questions. If you don't shoot first, the enemy will, and will stop you from performing the assignment. Usually, the leader knows more than the soldiers, and in the battle there is no time for questions and answers, only obedience.

On one occasion I had to leave a brother behind when going into former East Germany. He questioned every move I made and wanted to argue about it. His lack of cooperation turned out to be very costly for him. He asked, "Why didn't you warn me?" I tried many times, but he wouldn't listen or submit to authority, so he was left behind.

With our unit all together again we came up the stairs out of the subway tunnel onto the sidewalk next to the KGB Headquarters. We proceeded to walk around the headquarters thirteen times, praying and quoting the scriptures the Lord had given. Again, the Lord attended us with His presence and I know that angels were with us.

Kjell was the oldest member of the team, but remember, Jamie, the youngest member, walked with the staff. I hope God has heavenly videos, especially ones that show what is happening in the spiritual realm as you carry out God's assignments.

Back in the tunnel, we stopped in the spot directly under the KGB building. While praying, no one passed by for about twenty minutes. It was powerful and loud. Instead of stomping the rod on the walkway as an amen, Jamie stomped the ceiling of the tunnel toward the floor of the KGB.

We went to leave the tunnel, and at the exit the drunk man was sitting there. The blood had pretty well dried up and he wasn't hurt except for a scratch. A little blood can look like a great amount as it spreads.

Kjell then explained to the brothers that when God sends you on an assignment, the enemy often tries to thwart you by using a diversion. The man could have yelled for the police, claiming we pushed him down, and the assignment would have been canceled. Do not fall for the trick of the Devil, ". . . For we are not ignorant of his devices" (2 Corinthians 2:11).

Today, the former KGB Headquarters is a museum. The KGB has lost much of its power, and not only have many Jewish people gone to Israel, multitudes of people have been saved in the former USSR. The KGB no longer harasses as they did before and the statue of Dzerzinsky, its founder, has been removed.

Let God be praised.

CHAPTER 13
EUROCLYDON

Toward the end of 1988, my friend Kjell Sjöberg was impressed by the Lord to make trips to the four corners of the earth. According to Revelation 7:1, there are four angels standing at the four corners of the earth, holding back the four winds of the earth and the sea, until God accomplishes certain tasks.

Kjell asked if I would join him. At first, the work was to determine what the four corners of the earth were. How could anyone know? We certainly did not.

The plan was not to try to discover the corners, but to let God point them out. So we prayed. We asked the Lord for people to invite us to hold prayer conferences in four uttermost areas of the earth. There would be no solicitation on our part of any kind whatsoever. In addition, the invitations would be from people we had never met before. In a short time, four invitations from people we did not know arrived from four different areas of the world.

One of those invitations came from a small Eskimo (Inuit Native Indian) village in Nome, Alaska. Four churches there decided to hold a four-day prayer conference at the end of November, and the beginning of December 1989.

In Acts 1:8, Jesus said we would be witnesses to the ends of the earth from Jerusalem. Nome is definitely in the uttermost parts. With dog teams and snowmobiles as prevalent as pickup trucks for transportation, it makes for a very interesting place.

Years before, my daughter Lynn had bought me a down-filled coat that was good for temperatures to -70 degrees fahrenheit. I had never gotten to wear it until going to Nome, and was I ever thankful for that coat. That winter was especially cold. Temperatures dipped to -60 to -70 degrees fahrenheit during our entire stay in Fairbanks and Nome.

After meetings in Fairbanks our team flew to Nome. Previously, I had been to Alaska seven or eight times, but never to Nome. While on the airplane, I received a rather strange instruction from the Lord. He said, "Ask to meet the meanest man in Nome." Since none of us had met our hosting pastors, I wondered what they were going to think about us when I asked to meet the meanest man in Nome.

When we arrived, I was assigned to ride in the Assembly of God pastor's pickup. As we drove to Nome, I asked him about meeting the meanest man. Immediately he spoke out a name and drove me to one of his businesses located next to the "City of Sin Saloon". I had no idea what would happen; the Lord had just said to meet him.

This man made his living controlling the drug and prostitution trade in Nome. He was known for ripping off the Eskimos and profiting greatly from them by using alcohol. Once he was convicted of murder and served only a one day sentence. His wife had died the year before and part way through her funeral he got up and walked out, saying that he had to get back to work. The pastor driving me to meet him had conducted the funeral. He said she had met Jesus and was born again and had prayed for her husband up to the time of her death.

We entered the ivory store this man owned and the pastor introduced us. At that time we were living in Jerusalem, and the man asked me where I lived.

I told him, "Jerusalem."

He got up out of his chair and said very gruffly to me, "I would never go to Jerusalem, they would probably put me on a cross."

As he said that, the Holy Spirit rose up inside me so powerfully, when I opened my mouth and spoke, he was flung back by God and pinned against the wall. He couldn't move.

I simply said, "That would never happen. Jesus Christ was already put on the cross there for you."

Then stuttering, he spoke very mildly as he followed us out the door.

It did not take long for word to travel that Jesus was in town. That Thursday night the church was almost full as we began our prayer conference, there in a little corner of the world seemingly so insignificant.

I have learned that God can bring His plan to pass by many or by few (1 Samuel 14:6).

The venue is determined by the Lord.

During our prayer conferences we divided our time, using about 40% for the Word and 60% actually praying. I have been to prayer conferences where the time is spent speaking about prayer, even from the Word, but with very little time spent in prayer, if any.

We continued Friday morning and afternoon. We planned to have a meeting Saturday morning, flying by bush plane to a spot further west in the afternoon, then coming back for the evening meeting.

During the Friday evening service, one topic brought up for prayer was the Summit Conference between the United States and the Soviet Union. It was to be held the next day at the Island of Malta in the Mediterranean.

These two nations each brought a large naval ship to the island of Malta. Anchored offshore, President George Bush and President Mikhail Gorbachev would hold the Summit aboard the ships. A major point to be discussed concerned the USSR wanting the United States to stop pushing for the release of the Soviet Jews.

As we began to pray about this subject, God opened my sight into the spiritual realm (2 Kings 6:17). I prayed a very bold, prophetic prayer based upon what I saw in the Spirit. I prayed that the angels at the four corners of the earth who were holding back the winds and the sea would let go, and that such a violent storm would take place, the ships would be tossed to and fro. I also prayed the waters would be so rough, that the sailors aboard the anchored ships would be so sick they would be vomiting over the sides. Most of all, I prayed that the Summit would be canceled so the topic of the Soviet Jews could not even be spoken about.

Acts chapter 27 speaks of a great storm in this same region. The Apostle Paul was aboard a ship that ran into a southeast wind called "Euroclydon". He prophesied that the ship, its cargo, and many lives would be at stake and a shipwreck would happen, but that no lives would be lost. They shipwrecked on the Island of Malta, the same island where the Summit Conference was to be held.

Our dear brothers and sisters in Nome had not attended a prayer meeting quite like this before. They felt we were taking prayer into areas we had no place praying. They also questioned, who we thought we were to cancel a Summit Conference between the two most powerful nations on the earth? Most of them left and went to their homes very quickly.

The next morning, Saturday, only five or six people came to the prayer meeting. The others thought we had gone too far and thought we were very peculiar. Three of the pastors did not even come.

Around noon it was clear, crisp, and very cold as we went to the airport to take the short one-hour flight to the small Eskimo village of Wales. Our bush pilot had been attending the prayer conference and was quite reserved.

He flew us to Cape Prince of Wales on Seward Peninsula, the most western point on North America. We could see the Big and Little Diomede Islands, the big one belonging to the USSR with the small one belonging to the United States.

In the very small village of Wales was a little church, and after locating the pastor we went in to continue praying. Certainly we were at one end of the earth here.

During the flight back to Nome we wondered how many people would be in the church for the evening prayer meeting. When we arrived, we were shocked to see it filled to overflowing. The people were so excited and so on fire and expectant. What a difference from that morning!

They asked us if we had heard the news. We did not know of any news as we had made this short trip.

The people then told us to watch CNN News. A tremendous storm in the Mediterranean had taken place earlier in the day at the Island of Malta. It was so severe the Summit Conference between the United States and the USSR had to be canceled. No one could pass from ship to ship although the ships were anchored. The report also showed sailors so sick, they were vomiting over the side rails of both ships. Jesus had done it again! Consequently, the church was full. God is looking for those who will cooperate with Him in these end times.

At the Sunday morning service Kjell spoke, and I was to speak that evening. However, I had no message, so I looked forward to what God would do.

During the noon meal the pastor asked if any of us wanted to go snowmobiling. I had never been, and since I had my down coat, I went. What a blast; it was great fun. Since it was my first time I went slowly, maybe 25-30 miles an hour. Not so with my pastor friend, he was way ahead of me as we left Nome across the snow.

Some distance from town I came up a hill to a flat spot, and what I saw caused me to come to a full stop.

Again, the Lord by His grace opened my eyes into the spiritual realm. I saw two groups of angels standing in circles. In the middle stood two large angels, each with a list in his hand. Each would read his lists and point to one of the angels standing in the circle, and it appeared as though he gave that one instructions. I wanted to get closer to hear what was being said, but knew I was not supposed to. As I stood watching this, I knew something important was taking place. The angels were then sent forth into Nome. They walked up and down the streets and entered many of the houses. Not all, but certainly the ones they were told to.

I was so filled with joy and awe to see God's angels at one of the corners of the earth, just as the Bible says.

My friend saw that I was far behind and came back to me. When he looked at my face, he could not even ask a question. He knew I had seen something. We then returned to Nome.

Now I had something to say that evening. The blessing of the Lord came down upon us during the evening service. A nine-year old boy took the hand of his dad and they came forward and both were filled with the Holy Spirit. The man was our bush pilot from the day before. He was not quiet and reserved any longer as the tears of joy streamed down his face. Families came forward and God's blessings abounded. It was a night I shall never forget. "Behold, I send an Angel before you to keep you in the way and to bring you into the place which I have prepared" (Exodus 23:20).

The next morning we were leaving Nome, and unbeknownst to the team, Kjell had asked God for a sign showing we had accomplished everything the Lord sent us to do. He asked that before we flew out, someone would ask Jesus into their heart in a very unusual way, not in one of the meetings.

Early that Monday morning about six a.m., a pastor from Fairbanks who was a part of our team wanted a cup of coffee. We had used all the coffee from the place where we were staying, so he set out to find his cup of coffee.

He left through the back door to the alley just as an Eskimo man came walking by. Greeting him, the pastor asked where he could get a cup of coffee that early in the morning. The man introduced himself. His name was Mike, and he asked the pastor to join him as he was also going for coffee. At the restaurant Mike began to pour his heart out, not knowing the other man was a pastor.

Mike related how he could not sleep all night and he knew he had to get his life right with God, but did not know how. He said he was desperate and wanted to know if he could find God.

The pastor did not tell Mike anything except, "Yes, you can find God." He brought Mike back to where we were staying and told us about their conversation; he felt the leading of the Lord to have Kjell pray for Mike. We all joined in, and it was the best going-away present we ever received as Mike invited Jesus the Messiah into his heart.

Kjell then told us about his request and said this surely qualifies. Not often in an icebound village does an Eskimo walk up to someone and ask, "How do I get saved?"

It simply takes a person willing to humble himself, repent, and turn away from his sins, and ask Jesus to forgive his sins and invite Him to come into his heart. There is nothing greater than having a personal relationship with Jesus.

Again, the Lord had us in the right place at the right time. The enemies of Israel wanted to prevent the Soviet Jews from going to Israel, but God intervened and allowed us to participate.

Psalm 124: "If it had not been the LORD who was on our side," Let Israel now say— "If it had not been the LORD who was on our side, when men rose up against us, then they would have swallowed us alive, when their wrath was kindled against us; then the waters would have overwhelmed us, the stream would have gone over our soul; then the swollen waters would have gone over our soul." Blessed be the LORD, Who has not given us as prey to their teeth. Our soul has escaped as a bird from the snare of the fowlers; the snare is broken, and we have escaped. Our help is in the name of the LORD, Who made heaven and earth."

CHAPTER 14
BAGHDAD OR BUST

After almost two and one half years of preparation, the Holy Spirit Commando Team was in Finland for some days in 1987, preparing to make another strike into the city of Moscow for prayer warfare. God armed us not with missiles that you can see, but with spiritual missiles and spiritual hand grenades to toss in prayer to push back the kingdoms of darkness. These assignments were given by the Lord so that the Jews could leave the Soviet Union.

In the vision of 1974, that God by his grace allowed me to see, there was no Iron Curtain, there was no Berlin Wall; rather the Jewish people were walking out on highways built by God through prayer. One highway went through Finland into Scandinavia, the other one came out through Poland to Western Europe, into Germany, and into Holland. From those places the Jewish people got on ships and went home to Israel. The Lord said in order for this to happen we would have to go and prepare the way.

As we were preparing to go, while I was in prayer, the Holy Spirit gave me a very deep, deep impression.

He said, "Son, begin to prepare today to go to Iraq."

I said, "Iraq? Lord, we haven't even gotten to the Soviet Union on this trip! You're asking me already to prepare to go to Iraq?"

The Lord said, "Yes, it's going to be very vital and very important that you go, and I want you to go to Babylon."

I said, "Go to Babylon?" I thought, that's interesting, I don't know what that has to do with the Jews, but God, I know Your voice.

One thing I know, I know my God. I thank Him that He speaks. This is not a mystical testimony. Jesus said, when the Holy Spirit comes, He shall speak (John 16:13). He speaks about the things that point us to Jesus, and to things to come. So we shouldn't think it to be some strange thing, but it should be the testimony of every child of God, because Jesus says four times in John 10, "My sheep hear My voice."

I said, "Lord, if this is you, you will confirm your word to others in our group."

So I shared it with the group and they all had the same reaction I did.

They said, "Steven, stop! We haven't even gotten to Moscow and already you have us in Baghdad. That's a little quick, but we'll see what happens."

However, when we were on the airplane flying into Moscow, the newspaper delivered to us on the plane was *The Financial Times of London*. The first article on the inside front page—covering half the page—was about Saddam Hussein rebuilding the ancient city of Babylon. As all of us read it, we agreed that it was confirmation, that we believed God, and that we had better prepare ourselves to make the trip to Iraq. So for three years we made our preparations.

In 1989 the Lord spoke to us and said, "I want you in Iraq on May 28, 1990."

God's timing is absolutely perfect. His timing is exactly as important as the assignment.

Why the 28th of May? We didn't know, but the Lord did and we said, "Okay, Lord, we don't fully understand yet, but we will obey You."

Our travel arrangements were being prepared through an organization in Paris that handled tours into the Arab countries. Toward the end of April we finally received our documents to make the trip to Iraq. Then the company that did all the work for us went bankrupt, closed their doors, never to open again. We thought it was rather strange.

One obstacle I faced in going to Iraq was the issue of a visa. I couldn't submit my passport to get a visa into Iraq because of the Israeli stamps in it. I had a very difficult time trying to get a second passport.

When the travel documents were issued in Paris, I was speaking at a church in Berlin. An assistant pastor drove me to the American Consulate so I could get another passport. A lady there began screaming at me when I applied, and refused to even take the application. I laughed. My response made her hysterical. This didn't set well with her. I knew the enemy was behind the refusal. I asked to see the Consulate General and she yelled at me again and said "Leave." However, for me, it was Baghdad or Bust!

Back to the prayer closet. "Lord, what do I do?" In 1975, I received a Russian visa in Hamburg, Germany, which was supposed to be impossible to get from the Soviet Consulate. I was impressed to try the American Consulate in Hamburg; maybe I would be received there. Wrong!

I was yelled at there and told again, "No, you do not need a second passport."

This time I did not laugh. I walked out the door and started to walk down the street when I perceived the Holy Spirit very strongly telling me to go back in and try again. The man who yelled at me, the Vice Consular, wasn't behind the window this time; a German lady employee was. She listened to me, and by God's grace I had a copy of *EXODUS II* in the German language. She glanced through it, looked at the Israeli stamps in my passport and said,

"Ich bin ein Juden" — German for "I am a Jew."

Then in Hebrew, she said, "I need to cover for you, return in exactly two hours and speak only with me."

I left and returned two hours later. When I saw the man standing behind the window again my heart began to beat faster, but the Jewish lady motioned me over to another window. The Vice Consular started to come over to see what she was doing. But she spoke to him very sharply and he left us alone. She issued me my second passport, and out the door I went. I sent it by next day delivery to Judy in Seattle, along with my visa application. Judy sent it on to the Iraqi Embassy in Washington, D.C.

Back in the United States about two weeks later, I had heard nothing from the Iraqi Embassy. I finally called them on the telephone. The man said that he had my passport right in front of him. He asked me some questions and said it would take a few days, then he would put it in the mail. The problem was, I was leaving for Israel in two days, but I certainly couldn't tell him that. It was May 14, how could I get my passport and visa to Israel in time to go to Iraq? I would have to leave Israel on one passport—my first one—and enter Turkey on my second one, then continue on to Iraq with it, leaving my first one in Istanbul for safekeeping.

With the mail taking several days to arrive from Washington, D.C. to Seattle and the Embassy taking some more days, I had to trust God. Faith is a substance, a hope for things you can't see, Hebrews 11:1.

On the telephone, the man at the Iraqi Embassy asked, "What is this thick envelope in your packet?"

I replied, "Look and see."

He said it was a Federal Express prepaid overnight sack. Thank God my wife Judy had enclosed it with the application. She also hears from the Lord.

Phil Israelson flew from Seattle to Tel Aviv on May 20, and my passport arrived in Seattle the afternoon before. Judy gave it to Phil. And on May 21, 1990, we understood how critical the timing was.

On the 21st of May 1990, Saddam Hussein called a summit conference in Baghdad of all Arab nations. At this conference the only topic to be discussed was, "How the Arab nations have to stop the Jews of the Soviet Union from going to Israel." The conference was to begin on May 28, 1990.

In 1974, God gave a vision of the release of the Soviet Jews and said, "Go tell the people. Tell them that Jesus is coming again. When they see the Jews of the Soviet Union coming home, it means that I am announcing the return of my Son, Jesus the Messiah." Then in 1987, the Lord said to go to Babylon, present day Iraq, on May 28, 1990.

In 1990, on exactly the day that Saddam Hussein called the conference to prevent the Soviet Jews from coming home to Israel, there we were, the Holy Ghost Commando Team, entering Baghdad. On the 28th of May I had breakfast in Jerusalem, lunch in Istanbul, and dinner in Baghdad. If they had had any idea that I had any Jewish blood in me, and if they had known I had just come from Jerusalem, I doubt that I would be here writing this book. However, God is faithful. He goes before us. His Glory is our rear guard and He sends His angels before us. There isn't a thing Satan, Saddam, or anyone can do to one who obeys God and is led by His Holy Spirit. And so we went.

Saddam Hussein, on the 28th of May, shut down the whole nation of Iraq. It was closed to every single foreigner. No businessmen, no tourists, no one was allowed in. When we got on our airplane in Istanbul, we thought it strange that we were the only people on the airplane. When we landed at the big airport in Baghdad, we were the only ones in this absolutely huge, huge airport. It was amazing. Even the Iraqi's were amazed.

"What are you doing here?" They said, "Don't you know the whole nation is closed for anybody to enter?"

When we met our tour people they said, "Yes, you are the only people allowed in because the company that made your arrangements to come here went bankrupt, and we had no way to get in touch with any of you, so we allowed you to come in."

God is in control of everything!

It is a very momentous time in history in which we live. We are living during the fulfillment of prophecy written thousands of years ago. God chose you and me to live at this time to participate in what He is doing, to cooperate with Him.

Psalm 83: "Do not keep silent, O God! Do not hold Your peace, and do not be still, O God! For behold, Your enemies make a tumult, and those who hate You have lifted up their head. They have taken crafty counsel against Your people, and consulted together against Your sheltered ones. They have said, 'Come, and let us cut them off from being a nation, that the name of Israel may be remembered no more.' For they have consulted together with one consent; they form a confederacy against You. The tents of Edom and Ishmaelites; Moab and the Hagarites; Gebal, Ammon, and Amalek; Philistia with the inhabitants of Tyre; Assyria also has joined with them; they have helped the children of Lot. Selah. Deal with them as with Midian, as with Sisera, as with Jabin at the Brook Kison, who perished at En Dor, who became as refuse on the earth. Make their nobles like Oreb and like Zeeb, yes all their princes like Zebah and Zalmunna, who said, 'Let us take for ourselves the pastures of God for a possession.' O my God, make them like the whirling dust, like the chaff before the wind! As the fire burns the woods, and as the flame sets the mountains on fire, so pursue them with Your tempest, and frighten them with Your storm. Fill their faces with shame, that they may seek your name, O LORD. Let them be confounded and dismayed forever; yes, let them be put to shame and perish, that men may know that You, whose name alone is the LORD, are the Most High over all the earth."

Asaph, who wrote this so long ago, is speaking about those who would try to bring an end to this nation called Israel. The Bible is very clear about what God will do to anyone who tries to cut off Israel from being a people and being a nation. God said He is going to deal with them in this certain way. God has already set forth the judgment. He has already proclaimed it. We have read a part of that.

During the years Saddam Hussein has been president of Iraq, his number one aim has been to see the downfall and the annihilation of the nation of Israel and all Jewish people. When he fired his missiles at Israel during Desert Storm, he not only had the allied forces against him, he had another enemy. His name is the LORD GOD of Israel. God has been very faithful and true to His word.

Psalm 83 speaks about Edom, the Ishmaelites, Moab, the Hagarites, Gebal, Ammon, Amalek, Tyre, Assyria. These are places within the Middle East involving modern day Jordan, Iraq, and Lebanon. God prophesied that if they decide to annihilate Israel, indeed He would deal with them. He would burn them with flames and set the mountains on fire. He would pursue them; He would frighten them with His storm. Isaiah 21:1,5 tells of the fall of Babylon with the use of a "desert storm and shield".

When I left Seattle in 1973 with my family and moved to West Germany, I learned that God is a prophetic God. Everything that He does, He does prophetically. The things He had done in my life and in the lives of my family members, were to prepare us for the things that were to come. I saw His pattern of prophetic preparation in His word. Before the New Testament, we have the Old Testament, the prophetic preparation for what God is going to do. Before the New Covenant, the Old Covenant. Before Jesus came the first time, he sent another one to cry through the land to make straight the way, and his name was John the Baptist. He was the forerunner, the one to announce the coming of the Messiah.

The question I'd had of the Lord was, "Lord, I see that you do things prophetically. Lord, is there something that You are going to do to wake people up, to make them realize that indeed they are living in the last days? Is there something that You are going to do to announce the coming of Jesus the second time? Because You always do things prophetically. Is there something that You will do?"

I had no idea; it was just a question I had of the Lord. As I have mentioned, He answered that question in August 1974, when God by his grace allowed me to see a vision of the return of millions of Soviet Jews back to Israel.

Church, get ready. As you see the Jews return home to Israel, it is because Jesus the Messiah is coming soon. That is what God is announcing. He is looking for a people who will understand what He is doing and cooperate with Him for the return of the Messiah.

Micah 5:5, "When the Assyrian comes into our land, and when he treads our palaces, then we will raise against him seven shepherds and eight princely men. They shall waste with the sword the land of Assyria, and the land of Nimrod at its entrances; thus He shall deliver us from the Assyrian, when he comes into our land and when he treads within our borders. Then the remnant of Jacob shall be in the midst of many peoples." The Bible is talking about the Assyrian. Assyria is part of modern day Iraq. When the Assyrian becomes Israel's enemy, God raises against him seven shepherds and eight princely men.

On our team, there were seven pastors, or shepherds, and eight leaders going into the nation of Iraq, exactly as it is stated in Micah. The instructions were to waste the land of Assyria and the land of Nimrod with the sword at its entrances.

Micah 5:10-15: "'And it shall be in that day,' says the LORD, 'that I will cut off your horses from your midst and destroy your chariots. I will cut off the cities of your land and throw down all your strongholds. I will cut off sorceries from your hand, and you shall have no soothsayers. Your carved images I will also cut off, and your sacred pillars from your midst; you shall no more worship the work of your hands; I will pluck your wooden images from your midst; thus I will destroy your cities. And I will execute vengeance in anger and fury on the nations that have not heard.'"

The land of Nimrod is mentioned in Genesis 10. Nimrod built cities in what is now modern day Iraq. He built Babylon, Nineveh, Nimrod, Ur, and other cities. Nimrod is three generations removed from the flood. He is the son of Cush, who is the son of Ham, who is the son of Noah. As Nimrod built the city of Babylon, he began to build a tower called the Tower of Babel. Babylon introduced to humanity witchcraft and sorcery that has spread to the four corners of the earth. That is why God says in Micah 5:12, "I will cut off your sorceries." God was going to send fifteen men with a sword to go and to cut these things off. In 1989, the Holy Spirit again impressed me and said, "As I broke the back of Communism so quickly, even quicker am I going to break the back of Islam. You will preach the gospel of Jesus the Messiah from the black rock in Mecca, and multitudes of Moslems will come to know who Jesus is."

I saw a flash of lightning that went from Mecca in Saudi Arabia through to Indonesia, and multitudes of Moslems becoming disillusioned with their religion, and their desert god, Allah.

Allah is a desert god and leads his people only into desolation. Allah is not the Lord God of Israel. When Allah is referred to as "God" in the news media, do not be deceived, he is a desert god. Allah leaves his people desolate, with no hope and no life, because there is none in him. Only in Jesus is there life. God said to me, "I'm going to prepare multitudes of people worldwide who will step into the gap, who will preach the gospel to the hundreds of millions of Moslems worldwide."

Get ready; maybe God will call some of you. The Lord is preparing a people to serve Jesus, to respond to His call to go wherever and to do whatever He tells them to. When this will happen I do not know, but it will happen.

In Micah 5:13 God says, "Carved images, sacred pillars . . ." God says, I will bring my vengeance upon these. Saddam Hussein is searching far deeper than Islam for his sources of power. There are more images of Saddam Hussein in Iraq than there are people, and there are 17 million people. He has built statues of himself, some at least 90 feet tall. This goes absolutely against the Koran. And he has delved much deeper. Why? Islam began with Mohammed in Saudi Arabia, then spread to Iraq — the first nation to embrace it outside of Saudi Arabia. The demons of the Moslem faith were not powerful enough to overcome the Babylonian gods that have been there much, much longer. Saddam reaches deeper than Islam. He claims to be a direct descendant of Nebuchadnezzar, even his very offspring.

Not only does Saddam Hussein believe that he is a direct descendant of Nebuchadnezzar, meant to destroy Israel and to annihilate the Jewish people, his hero is a man by the name of Saladin, Sultan of Egypt and Syria. Saladin led the Turks to battle in Israel at a place called the "Horns of Hittan" in 1187 A.D., and destroyed the Crusader armies there. Because he did that, Saddam Hussein believes he can destroy all the Allied forces that are against him because he will do the same thing that Saladin did.

Before the war of "Desert Storm", Iran and Iraq fought an 8 1/2 year war. One thing we noticed walking through the cities of Iraq, was that there was a whole section of the population missing. It was approximately from the ages of 18 to 25. Many died in the war between Iraq and Iran. Over one million people were killed in that war. Where was the protection of Allah?

The seeds of witchcraft, sorcery, false religions, Greek gods, all mythology, Roman gods, Scandinavian gods and shamanism that have come to native peoples around the world were all disseminated from ancient Iraq.

Nimrod came from ancient Iraq. He was the first man to put walls around cities. He was the first man to want a one world government, and the first to set himself up as a god to be worshiped. This is another source from which Saddam Hussein is drawing his strength and evil power.

Genesis 10:8 — "Cush begot Nimrod; he began to be a mighty one on the earth. He was a mighty hunter before the LORD; therefore it is said, 'Like Nimrod the mighty hunter before the LORD.' And the beginning of his kingdom was Babel, Erech, Accad, Calneh, in the land of Shinar. From that land he went to Assyria and built Nineveh, Rehoboth, Ir, Calah, and Resen between Nineveh and Calah (that is the principal city)."

This man Nimrod was known as a mighty one on the earth. He killed some kind of serpent. Historians are not sure; they don't know what kind of serpent he killed, but it must have been something that caused great fear in his time, for they made him king. He wasn't satisfied being king; he wanted to be God. We read in Genesis 11 that he began to build the Tower of Babel. As he is rebuilding Babylon, Saddam is trying to draw strength from Nimrod's example.

The Babylonian spirit is very seductive and strong. The Rolling Stones music group had a worldwide tour in 1997 and 1998, called "Bridges to Babylon". Recently, I saw a bumper sticker on a car in Seattle, Washington, that said, "If you start something, you've done too much, groovy times in Babylon." The symbol of the EEC in Europe for the 1990s is the tower of Babel. The world is caught up with the spirit of Babylon.

Nimrod, according to Jewish scholars, is called a mighty hunter of the souls of men. He forced people to worship him. He wanted to be worshiped as God. Because of this precedent, we can begin to understand other kings, such as Hummarabi, Nebuchadnezzar, and the latest whom we have in our own time—Saddam

Hussein—wanting to set themselves up as gods. He has said it openly. He said it while we were in Baghdad at the end of the conference in May 1990. He said, "I have enough fire power to obliterate half of Israel off the face of the map and I have enough chemical weapons to kill the other half." From his missiles and by his actions, we could see that Saddam's real purpose was to try to bring forth the destruction of the children of Israel. However, the Bible says, "He who keeps Israel shall neither slumber nor sleep" (Psalm 121:4). There was not one direct death from the SCUD missiles Saddam fired into Israel. Three people had heart attacks, but as far as direct hits from the SCUD missiles, not one death. They became "dud" missiles. Of the thirty-nine missiles fired at Israel, two went to Haifa.

God has graciously enabled my wife and me to help employ Soviet Jews in Israel. We have worked with Messianic believers who own companies there to employ Soviet Jews. One of the factories is in Haifa. The first SCUD missile that went to Haifa landed 400 yards from the factory that employed Soviet Jews, but not even a window was broken in this factory. So, God is faithful. The second and last SCUD missile that went to Haifa landed 200 yards from the apartment complex that housed Soviet Jews who worked in this factory, with no damage to the apartment building.

Jesus is certainly faithful to His Word. He is not sleeping. He is not slumbering.

CHAPTER 15
HONOLULU, IRAQ

After clearing customs at the Baghdad airport we met our guide, Mohammed Ali.

When we met our bus driver, he pretended not to know English in order to spy on us, assuming we wouldn't guard our speech. On the way to our hotel, Mohammed told us that we couldn't travel around much for three days because of the Arab Summit Conference. He addressed us as archeology students. We found out why later.

Our arrangements were handled by a member of our team in France. Since he had a PhD and we only applied to go to the ancient ruins, Iraqi authorities assumed it was in archaeology. Therefore, they assumed we were all archaeologists.

During the bus ride from the airport to the hotel it became very apparent to several team members that we spoke many Christian words. A religious jargon, so to speak. Some refer to it as "Christianeze". We knew we had to set up code words, as sometimes even walls seemed to have ears. I had found this out during my travels in Eastern Europe before the Iron Curtain came down. You never knew if hotel rooms were bugged.

So we constructed code words that would not reveal who we were. The Holy Spirit is very witty, and I am sure He gave us much inspiration.

At the hotel we paired up to share rooms, then each team took a one-hour shift of intercession, so we would be covered in prayer during the night hours. During the day hours we were together and prayed as a group. Much of the prayer was in the Spirit, no one but God could understand those words. But prayer in our native tongues had to be in new code words.

Once while talking with Mohammed I spoke the name "Saddam Hussein".

Mohammed became very fearful and agitated, telling me very strongly, "Never mention that name out loud again!"

He then looked around to see if anyone had overheard us. I had become accustomed to this during my travels in the USSR. Russians would never speak the name of their leader aloud, afraid someone would overhear and report them to the police. Only through fear, intimidation, bodily harm, or imprisonment can a dictator stay in power.

Our code name for Saddam Hussein was inspired by the Book of Esther. Haman's conspiracy to kill all the Jews provided our code. So we called Hussein "Hey-Man".

We could not pray aloud about the Summit Conference so we called it "The Midianites". Israel was coded with "Michael's Land" because Michael is the archangel of the Jewish people. "Michael's Friends" were the Jewish people.

We met some people from Operation Mobilization, a missionary organization, who were in Iraq for a few weeks. We called them the "Orange Marmalades", for OM.

When we went to visit ancient Nineveh in Northern Iraq, we were given an unscheduled stop for the afternoon. Mohammed took us to a very large Kurdish city. We couldn't refer to the people there as Kurds in our speech because Saddam Hussein hated the Kurdish people. He used chemical weapons on one Kurdish town, gassing and killing over 5,000 men, women, and children.

Saddam Hussein did this in one of his own cities; what will he do to others? Our code name for the Kurds was "Cottage Cheese". Whenever we referred to cottage cheese, all our team members knew whom we were talking about or praying for.

Our all-night prayer times and other gatherings gave us much opportunity to intercede and pray concerning the "Midianites". Jesus said about the Holy Spirit in John 16:13, "...and He will tell you things to come." Therefore, we kept a prayer log to pass on to the next team the things the Lord impressed upon us in prayer. Over and over the Lord revealed to us the agendas for every meeting of the summit conference. We were able to pray with knowledge and understanding (Psalm 111:10), enabling us to launch our spiritual missiles to stop the Arab nations from reaching any unity and from accomplishing their goals before they met each day.

In the evenings we gathered for our corporate prayer times. However, we first tuned in to the BBC, as each night the answers to our prayers were reported. It was exciting to see how the exact things we prayed for were totally canceled from the conference. The "Midianites" could not come to agreement. Saddam Hussein was so angry that his goal of blocking the Soviet Jews would not be met; he declared that he had the fire power to blow half of Israel off the map, and enough chemical weapons to kill the other half.

During one of these nights, the Holy Spirit told my roommate that the PLO was going to attack Israel the next afternoon by sea. We alerted the other teams and prayed until we had the assurance that all would be okay. Sure enough, we heard on the BBC broadcast that four boats financed by Col. Muammar Qadhafi, dictator of Libya, had tried to enter a beach at Tel Aviv, but were caught by the Israeli Navy. God showed us what to pray for, how to pray, and when to pray. He is the Leader and there is tremendous power in prayer. The very course of history can be affected through prayer.

We need to be a praying Church. I have a pastor friend in Berlin who gauges the size of his church by the number of people attending the all-night Friday prayer meetings. On one occasion I was there when he rebuked his congregation because only 600 people had been at the Friday night prayer meeting. He has over twice that number in his congregation.

On our first tour outside the city of Baghdad, Mohammad Ali took us to a ziggurat. Ziggurats are ancient pyramid-like temples. The ziggurats have stairways which lead up to altars. According to many scholars, the Tower of Babel could very well have been the model for ziggurats. They are manmade and contain altars where sacrifices were made to idols. There are many such ziggurats in Iraq. The first one we saw was made of layered bricks. Because of wind erosion it had many holes, so birds had made their nests there. Mohammed asked us to be very quiet when approaching the ziggurat. Then he explained that if we all shouted the same word, it would be quite a sight to see the birds fly out of their holes.

As a group, we had one word that was spoken over and over again because we didn't have a code word for it. That word was "Hallelujah". It would slip out constantly. So I proposed a word to shout at the birds, which could also be code for "Hallelujah". I explained to Mohammed that each state in the United States has a capital city, and the state of Hawaii . . . and he interrupted me, saying, "I know, Honolulu!" So we all yelled "Honolulu" and from then on he referred to us as the "International Honolulu Team". We found ourselves constantly using "Honolulu" as a praise word and Mohammed also began to say it.

As I stated previously, I believe Saddam Hussein is re-building Babylon, thinking he can draw strength and power from it. If he receives any power at all, it will be demonic power. He has built statues of himself, some 90 to 100 feet tall, and millions of his pictures are located throughout Iraq. Although the Koran strictly forbids Moslems from doing this, the Babylonian powers are stronger than the demonic powers behind Islam.

Saddam patterns himself after Nebuchadnezzar, and Revelation 17 and 18 tells us that one of the last end-time battles will be against the spirit of Babylon.

Babylon is very powerful and will fall in one hour. The influence of the spirit of Babylon is worldwide and it will fall, but only at the direction of the Lord. The Lord is giving the strategy and the order for it to happen. Anyone attempting to engage the spirit of Babylon to battle in prayer warfare before the correct time, is very unwise and will suffer greatly.

As powerful, exciting, and purposeful as the trip to Iraq was, after returning home to our various countries, many of us came under severe attack. My brothers and I experienced horrendous battles against ourselves, our families, and our ministries. A few days after returning home, one brother's wife gave birth to a stillborn child. It was devastating. Thank God the Lord believes in restoration. After returning from Iraq, I was restored over a period of five years in my life, my marriage, and my family. Some team members became sick, and I could go on about others. The point is, the closer we come to the return of Jesus, the more trouble Satan is going to try to cause. We must keep ourselves under the protection of the Lord. This is accomplished by being obedient to the Lord. Jesus learned obedience through the things He suffered (Hebrews 5:8).

In 1996, three of us who had been part of the Iraqi team met together to pray and ask the Lord to show us what we had done to remove His protection from us, thus opening us to the attack of the enemy. We reconstructed each day's events from our diaries and memories. We found the one event that had troubled every one of our spirits. We had never spoken about it before, because we hadn't obeyed the prompting of the Holy Spirit in us at the time it happened. When the Lord showed us the act which He had not instructed us to do, we repented with godly sorrow. As we shared this with some other team members, each one knew in his heart exactly what the event was and when the disobedience occurred.

Toward the end of our days in Iraq, when we were next to the walls of ancient Babylon, we held a communion service. This service was planned; however, we had to make it look like a picnic. At first Mohammed said, "NO!" But we showed him our itinerary that said we were to have a picnic at the walls of Babylon. To ensure our case, we purchased fruit and bread beforehand. Mohammed finally agreed, and to any passerby it seemed as if we were having a picnic.

Being one of the leaders of this trip, I can say that everything we did corporately up to that point was discussed among the leadership in detail, except one point of the communion service. At the end, the pastor leading the communion instructed one man to take the cup and pour out what was remaining at the various gates of Babylon and the floor of Nebuchadnezzar's throne room. A second brother joined him. This pouring out was not discussed, and I knew in my spirit it was wrong, but I didn't say anything. I have now learned my other brothers also had a check in their spirits. What we did was wrong, it opened all of us to attack, and it has been costly.

Why didn't we speak up and stop this pouring out of the cup from the communion? Each one of us had doubts like, "Who am I?" "What's wrong with me?" "Maybe that brother knows something I don't know?" Consequently, we didn't obey the prompting of the Holy Spirit. The spirit of anti-Christ and of anti-anointing stopped us. We didn't trust the anointing of Jesus Christ within us and listened to doubts promoted by the enemy because the mystery of lawlessness was at work (2 Thessalonians 2:7). The anti-Christ spirit makes you quiet; it causes you to even doubt your calling. It works when lawlessness is present, and Jesus said in the last days lawlessness would abound (Matthew 24:12).

About eight to nine months before the trip to Iraq, the pastor (who led the communion) and I heard about different prayer groups pouring out communion wine on the ground as an act of spiritual warfare. Neither one of us had a witness in our spirits that this was a correct thing to do. Ecclesiastes 9:18 says, "Wisdom is better than weapons of war, but one sinner destroys much good." Strongs Concordance describes this sinner as "a person through his actions can cause harm, loss; to forfeit, miss, condemn and lead astray; or to sin, destroying much good, in the widest sense, even of others". A reckless person, one operating outside God's wisdom, can stop the bearing of fruit or cut off fruit, so that it does not remain. In John 15:16, Jesus says you should bear fruit and that your fruit should remain (not <u>shall</u> remain) but SHOULD. Then whatever you ask the Father in the name of Jesus, He may give you.

The spirit of Babylon is a seducing spirit. It is very strong and has trapped the whole world. Its wine numbs the senses, even those of Christians. It works by flattery, causing people to seek experiences and thrills. But most of all it seduces, like a harlot, trying to make us fornicate with her, TO ROB US OF OUR INTIMACY WITH JESUS CHRIST.

Those who drink the wine that Babylon has to offer kill the fruit of the Spirit, and they have no love one for another. They want experiences and more experiences. To get them, people become intoxicated until their hearts are enslaved (Hosea 4:11). The wine from Babylon deteriorates the boundaries of a person's life. It is a slow process but when complete, the people don't even realize what has taken place. When boundaries fall, the seduction comes, and Babylon, the mother of harlots and abominations, rules in their lives (Revelation 17:5).

In Proverbs chapters 1-15, wisdom, the simple or seduced ones, and harlots are mentioned over and over again. We need intimacy with Jesus and God's wisdom to establish boundaries to keep the seducing spirit of Babylon out of our lives. God's wisdom will keep us sober and effective to be instruments of righteousness so that we can cooperate with God in seeing His end-time purposes and plans accomplished. People who base their Christianity on experience alone have been deceived and seduced by the spirit of Babylon. Revelation 18:4 says, "Come out of her, my people."

God's wisdom ". . . from above is first pure, then peaceable, gentle, willing to yield, full of mercy and good fruits, without partiality and without hypocrisy.

Now the fruit of righteousness is sown in peace by those who make peace" (James 3:17-18).

I believe Peter, the apostle of Jesus Christ, summed it up well in 1 Peter 4:7-8: "But the end of all things is at hand; therefore be serious and watchful in your prayers. And above all things have fervent love for one another, for love will cover a multitude of sins." This is God's wisdom.

Dear ones, great end-time battles are before us. They will be fought with the strategy provided by the Lord and in the order the Lord directs. Before that great city of Babylon is made desolate, becoming nothing in one hour (Revelation 18:10,19), God will show how the merchants—i.e. the Philistines, the Canaanites, Jericho, the Assyrians, Jezebel, Leviathan, among others—which are spirits will be defeated through the release of many special anointings of the Holy Spirit. If you do not understand this, I recommend you do not engage the spirit of Babylon in prayer.

CHAPTER 16
EVIAN-LES-BAINS

One day my friend Gustav Scheller asked me, "Steve, do you know what happened in 1938 at Evian-les-Bains, France?"

I replied, "I have never even heard of Evian, France, so how could I know what happened there? Besides, I was born in 1939."

Gustav began to tell me about a conference held in Evian during July 1938. I was so shocked with what he told me, I had to research it for myself.

My major at university was European History. I searched my old textbooks and could not find one single entry recorded about this conference. Finally, I got the information from the archives of the Library of Congress.

In 1933 Adolph Hitler, an Austrian, came to power as Chancellor of Germany. He had written a book called *Mein Kampf.* In it, he tells of his struggles, his philosophy about politics, and his plan to annihilate the Jewish people so a master race could be established. His Aryan race would be tall, blond, with blue eyes, although he was short, with dark hair and dark eyes. He called for the Germans to establish the so-called Third Reich.

Paramount to his plan was the extermination of the Jewish race. He believed he had a mandate to do this and it was one reason he came to power.

During 1933, Hitler very slowly began to eliminate the rights of the Jewish people in Germany, just as he wanted to eliminate the Jews themselves. As his power increased, he took away more and more rights. They were taken away a few at a time. He did not take their rights away all at once, that would have been too obvious. He simply took a little here and a little there, until 1938. During the period 1933-1938, concentration camps were established in Sachsenhausen, Esterwegen, Colombia Haus (Berlin), Buchenwald, and Dachau.

The "Anschluss", the annexation of Austria into the Third Reich, occurred in 1938. There was almost no resistance. Then overnight, Hitler did in Austria what took him five years to do in Germany. He took away all the rights of the Jewish people, confiscating their businesses and instituting his atrocities immediately.

The impotent League of Nations tried to do something, but failed miserably. The League stood for human rights; however, when it came to the Jewish people, it did nothing for them. In February 1938, the League discontinued their meager efforts. Only private Jewish organizations continued to help Jews in Germany.

When Hitler annexed Austria into Germany, the plight of the Jews was related to Franklin Roosevelt, President of the United States.

When the evidence concerning the Jews was shown to President Roosevelt, he called a meeting of the nations of the world. This meeting was for the express purpose of rescuing the Jewish people out of Germany and Austria. He called for the conference because the League of Nations had failed.

Evian, France, was chosen as the venue. It is a small town located on the shore of Lake Geneva directly across from Lausanne, Switzerland. A very large well-known hotel, where other diplomatic meetings had taken place, was selected.

Thirty-two of the nations invited answered the call of President Roosevelt.[2] On the 6th of July, 1938, fifteen weeks after Hitler had taken Austria, these nations came together. The question before them was, "How do we rescue the Jewish people out of Germany and Austria?"

The first hours of this conference, which turned into two full days, were spent arguing about who would chair the conference. Losing interest halfway through the conference, many of the delegates went out skiing or boating on Lake Geneva. Evidently recreation was more important than aiding the Jewish people. Therefore, most of the conference time was already consumed.

During the conference it was reported by the *London Times* that in Vienna, Austria, thousands of Jews were lined up in front of British, American, and other embassies. They were trying to get visas to escape Hitler's oppression. However, all embassy officials told the Jews to wait for the outcome of the conference at Evian. It would then be decided what to do with the Jewish people.[3]

Finally, after two days of arguing, the United States of America was chosen to chair the remaining few hours of this conference.

The representative from the United States was given the position of ambassador by President Roosevelt. The representative's title was The Honorable Myron C. Taylor, Ambassador on Special Mission. Each representative sent to the conference was at the ambassador level or higher. Some were even cabinet members in their nation's governments. Evian hosted a very powerful group of diplomats.

Myron Taylor from the United States stood up. After thanking France for hosting the conference he declared, "We all understand and know that this problem is so vast. However, there is nothing we are going to be able to do for these refugees at this conference. We, the United States of America, will not take another single Jewish person beyond our present quota."[4]

With that shocking opening statement from the United States, nation after nation echoed similar sentiments. The overwhelming conclusion of the conference was, "We do not want the Jews."

Lieutenant-Colonel the Hon. T.W. White, D.F.C., V.D., M.P., Minister for Trade and Customs from Australia said, "We do not have a racial problem and we will not import one."[5]

From Canada, the second largest land mass country on the face of the earth, with one of the fewest populations, Mr. Hume Wrong, Permanent Delegate to the League of Nations, said, "Our nation isn't big enough to bring in any more immigrants."[6] A second and even more incriminating statement followed later, "None are too many."

Ireland said that because of the depression they just did not have the ability to take any Jews.[7]

Three nations did volunteer to take a small number of Jews. The Dominican Republic 500, then Holland and Denmark said they could take 4,500, for a total of 5,000 Jewish people. Later, not even these nations would take in Jews.

When I read the official transcripts of the Evian Conference, I wept. Not just because of the rejection of the Jews, but also because of man's inhumanity to man, and the consequences facing those nations according to Genesis 12:3. "And I will curse him who curses you." These nations brought on themselves a curse. They went against God. What arrogance from the nations. Isaiah 40:15,17 says, "Behold, the nations are as a drop in a bucket, and are counted as the small dust on the balance; . . . All nations before Him are as nothing, and they are counted by Him less than nothing and worthless." Psalm 2:1,2,4: "Why do the nations rage, and the people plot a vain thing? The kings of the earth set themselves, and the rulers take counsel together, against the LORD and against His Anointed, . . . He who sits in the heavens shall laugh; the LORD shall hold them in derision."

How would the nations be cursed?

A plan was proposed by George Rublee, director of the Intergovernmental Committee, asking one half of the nations represented at Evian to take 25,000 Jewish people each. If sixteen nations had done so, every single Jewish person would have been rescued out of Germany and Austria.[8]

Had this plan had been implemented, would there have been a holocaust? Would there have been a World War II?

However, the nations said "No." And yet many nations had taken refugees over the years. The United States alone had opened its borders to 585,000 refugees from Cuba, and many thousands of Vietnamese boat people. But to 25,000 Jews, along with other nations, the United States said "NO."

Who was behind this mass rejection? Ultimately, it was Satan. He was engaging in spiritual battle to influence the nations to reject the Jews. Satan again wanted every single Jewish person killed. He wanted to thwart God's plan. If he had succeeded, the Bible, the Word of God, would have been desecrated and it could have been said that God did not protect His people, and was not powerful enough to bring forth His prophetic plan.

Hitler had spies in Evian. When the Jewish people were rejected by the nations, it was reported to Berlin. Those spies said, "You can do anything you want to the Jews, the whole world does not want them." One German newspaper declared: "Jews For Sale, Who Wants Them? No One."

The Nazis tried to get the nations at Evian to take the Jews by selling them. The Gestapo forced a famous Jewish surgeon, Dr. Professor Heinrich Benda from

Vienna, to take the Nazi plan to Evian. He was instructed to offer for sale the Jewish people of Germany and Austria to the nations. The price tag was $250 per Jew. If he did not get the money, the first 40,000 Jews would be sent to the concentration camps. A true documentary was made about Professor Benda's trip entitled "The Mission to Evian" by a Hungarian film maker. Professor Benda was born in Hungary. This documentary, distributed by Daniel Film, Munich, details some proceedings of the conference. It shows how he was laughed at, scorned, and finally thrown out. Under no circumstances were the nations, nor the churches, going to help the Jews.

After the Evian Conference, on August 17, 1938, a ship, with fifty-three Jewish people, left Hamburg, Germany, for Helsinki, Finland. The Jews aboard had all the necessary documents, passports, and visas to go to other nations, but they were not allowed to disembark in Helsinki. On the ship there was a pregnant Jewish woman who went into labor when the ship docked. She was taken to a hospital where she delivered her baby, at which time they were taken back to the ship immediately. The ship returned to Hamburg and those Jewish people, including the newborn child, were taken to concentration camps, to die at the hands of the Nazis. Finland was not represented at the Evian Conference. However, Finland went along with the decision of the other nations to reject the Jewish people.[9]

Another ship, the St. Louis, with approximately 900 Jews on board sailed for New York after Evian. They were denied permission to disembark at Ellis Island where before multitudes of immigrants had entered the United States. The reason? The U.S. Government had declared at Evian that they would not take any more Jewish people than their quota. The ship sailed on to Quebec City, Canada, where again they were not allowed to disembark. The ship returned to Germany and the Jewish people were sent to concentration camps where most died.

Indeed, the world did not want the Jewish people. Hitler considered this to be a stamp of approval from the nations for his plans concerning the Jews. He could go ahead and annihilate them; after all, who would care?

On the night of November 9-10, 1938, Kristallnacht (Crystal Night) happened in Germany. This was when the windows of synagogues, Jewish businesses, and homes were smashed and the Holocaust went into full swing. Hitler, the Nazis, and the Germans are not the only ones to blame for the Holocaust. What about the nations that met at Evian? Where was the church during this time? Where were the intercessors?

Isaiah 59:16 says, "He saw that there was no man, and wondered that there was no intercessor." Ezekiel 22:30 says, "So I sought for a man among them who would make a wall, and stand in the gap before Me on behalf of the land, that I should not destroy it; but I found no one."

Where was the church? What were we doing? God help us! Ultimately, the responsibility lies with the church and the intercessors.

The Christian churches did little to help, some individuals, yes. However, most failed to register their objection. They did not protest to Hitler or Germany against Nazi atrocities to the Jewish people. They did not condemn such evils.

Not long after the Evian Conference, the world was plunged into a war. The very nations that rejected the Jews were at war and the casualties were very high. Since then, abortions have been legalized worldwide. Over 35,000,000 just in the United States alone. I really wonder who is having a Holocaust now? How many sons and daughters have to die before the church wakes up?

I am concerned because we are living in the midst of Bible prophecy being fulfilled right before our eyes. The Jews from the former Soviet Union are going to Israel. Yet, where is the church and where are the intercessors? I know some Christians and a few churches are involved, but what are many others doing?

Zechariah 12:3 says all nations will turn against the Jews, Jerusalem, and Israel. But there is one nation that should not, and that is the "holy nation" (1 Peter 2:9).

An unprecedented wave of evangelism is about to occur worldwide when the Jewish people from all countries go to Israel. It is God's intention this time that the church and the intercessors, the Christians, be involved. God wants to bless those who bless the Jewish people. The "holy nation" must not turn its back on the Jewish people this time through compromise or a self-setting agenda. The question, "Am I my brother's keeper?" (Genesis 4:9) had better already be settled and answered in the hearts of Christians.

From June 29, 1988, through the first week of July, a conference was organized. The first half was held in Berlin, Germany. The second half was held in Evian-les-Bains, France.

The desire of the organizing committee was, for every nation represented at the Evian Conference of 1938, to send intercessors to this conference held fifty years later. Other nations that had, during their history, rejected Jewish people were also encouraged to send intercessors.

Christians from forty-three nations came to "Berlin'88". First of all, with the desire to repent for rejecting the Jewish people. I had the privilege of being a part. Secondly, to be reconciled with the Jews. Thirdly, to intercede for the Soviet Jews' release, in order to go to Israel. Fourthly, we prayed for the return of all Jews, worldwide, to Israel.

A work of the Holy Spirit happened in our hearts when we had a Divine visitation during the time of repentance. It started with the Jewish contingent from Israel asking forgiveness from the Germans and the other nations for harboring bitterness. It was not orchestrated, it came from their hearts and was inspired by the Holy Spirit. Then representatives from nation after nation, from their hearts broke forth into prayer. It was some of the most anointed praying I have ever participated in. They asked God and the Jewish people present to forgive them for anti-Semitism and for rejecting and persecuting them.

Also attending were Jews from Germany. Initially they simply observed, but as the conference continued they felt the sincere repentance of the delegates.

The reconciliation that took place between the nations and the Jewish people was necessary because the nations had failed to rescue them. The reconciliation with survivors of the Holocaust was especially powerful.

I personally believe that God would have preferred to establish the State of Israel on the prayers of intercessors, rather than upon the blood and lives of six million Jews lost in the Holocaust. Where were the intercessors? God's blessing would have come. Instead, the world brought a curse upon itself for rejecting the Jews at Evian in 1938. The world received World War II. Even today, some nations that attended Evian suffer with great problems. Cuba, Nicaragua, Honduras, and others are still living through terrible tragedy.

When I was a student in grammar school, the sun never set on the British Empire. Where is the "great" in Great Britain today?

The deterioration of society in the United States of America; the abortions, and the plight of "Generation X" are just some of its problems. The list goes on and on.

"But GOD!" God listens to the intercessors as they pour out their hearts before Him. During the times of corporate prayer in Berlin the intercession was so powerful, we could not stop the meetings. The 24-hour prayer room was always jammed with so many people praying that others had to stand out in the hall. Wherever you went in the Congress Hall in Berlin, many of the more than 2,000 delegates were huddled in prayer groups.

We chose Berlin to begin this conference for several reasons. It was still a divided city in 1988. The Berlin Wall was still in place then. The Iron Curtain still hung, dividing Europe into East and West. This was the city of Hitler's power. It had held the infamous "Wannsee Conference" where Hitler proposed his "final solution" to what he called the "Jewish problem". His solution was to totally annihilate the Jewish people. He believed the whole world would thank him for it and make him "Der Fuhrer" of the world. That is why he had the Holocaust so well documented with photographs; he thought the nations would worship him.

Certainly Germany was guilty of the act of commission, actually committing the Holocaust. However, it was not the only nation responsible. The other nations washed their hands of the Jewish people, committing the sin of omission, and therefore were equally guilty for the Holocaust.

That was why we were having this conference.

Each day during the meetings different conference leaders led some participants to pray at the Berlin Wall. While we were having our meetings in West Berlin, about 700 Christians from East Germany were meeting in East Berlin. They had groups marching and praying along the Berlin Wall at the same time we did. The Wall did not stand a chance.

Since I had lived in West Germany in 1973, joining my prayers with multitudes of others' prayers, I had prayed at the Berlin Wall many times before. This time I was privileged to be with 300 intercessors on the west side of the Wall, while a couple of hundred intercessors led by Dr. Paul Toaspern were on the east side. We walked and prayed for about four hours along the Berlin Wall. Then a small group went with Judy and me to meet Paul Toaspern, his wife, and some East German believers.

I had met Paul and his family in Hungary during the summer of 1976, and we became very good friends. He was a Lutheran pastor. At the end of World War II, while living in West Germany, the Lord told him there were not many pastors in East Germany. Paul and his wife prayed and they knew they had to move to East Germany with their seven children to minister there. They knew full well the persecution for the entire family would be horrible, but with God's help they went. He became Director of Evangelism of the Landeskirche, the State Church of East Germany. His books and voice, containing the prophetic words the Lord gave him, were uncompromising and were like arrows in the sides of the communist and apostate church leaders of East Germany. He had been arrested on many occasions and had seen terrible things done to his family. And yet he was filled with the love of Jesus like no other man I have ever met.

We prayed together and the presence of God was so powerful. We made it back to West Berlin just in time for the final meeting.

The next morning, a contingency of Berlin'88 people boarded a double-decker bus and other means of transportation to head for Evian-les-Bains, France. We would conclude with a three-day conference in Evian.

The small Jewish community of Evian extended an invitation to us to have our final meeting in their synagogue. We had invited them to attend our times of intercession and a small number came, partly out of curiosity I suspect.

These meetings were held exactly fifty years later on the same days as the 1938 Evian Conference. We did not know whether or not this 50-year anniversary would bring forth a jubilee or not, but we asked the Lord to reconcile us with the Jews of Evian.

The few who attended our small conference were touched by the repentance and intercession. On the Friday afternoon before Shabbat, or Sabbath, began, they invited us to the synagogue.

Meanwhile, Johannes Facius and I went to the actual hotel where the 1938 conference was held in Evian, and asked if we could rent a meeting room for about one hour. After telling the manager of this stately hotel why, he said absolutely not. However, that did not stop us. We had the delegates find their way to the hotel several at a time. We filled up the outdoor coffee shop tables and drank coffee. But more importantly, we prayed right there on the grounds.

Friday, the third day we were in Evian, we made our way to the small synagogue. Evian is not a large place, so the synagogue was not very large either. A very famous water source comes from here, Evian water, and is sold around the world. We were asking for the water of the Holy Spirit to be present.

During the 1938 Conference, Golda Meir led a group of Jewish people to Evian to present a paper to the delegates. They did not allow her to. She was not allowed to say even one single word. In Berlin and also in Evian, we had Jewish people with us, they were always given the first words.

There was an old rabbi, and with him came elderly Jews. The rabbi greeted us and reserved the time for any remarks he would make for the end; he didn't want to say anything at the beginning. After all, he did not know what we were going to do. He turned the meeting over to us.

First, we began by singing songs in Hebrew. Then people from the various nations stood and asked for forgiveness from the bottoms of their hearts. I cannot explain what happened in all of our hearts that day in July 1988 inside the synagogue at Evian. These elderly Jews had gone through the Holocaust because our nations had refused to help them. Yet here those very nations were asking for forgiveness, and it was overwhelming to say the least. I do not think there was a dry eye in the place.

When we were finished, the rabbi rose and said, "I cannot call you ladies and gentlemen. I must call you brothers and sisters."

If you have ever been in a place where the Holy Spirit invaded your midst, you can understand what happened in that synagogue.

The rabbi shared what happened to him during the

Holocaust, how he was mistreated and lost every single member of his family in Nazi concentration camps. He stated, "I have seen a demonstration of something here today that I never thought would ever be possible. Something has happened in my heart today."

There were no cameras present that day to record the people repenting, asking for forgiveness and being reconciled. However, I know it is recorded forever, in Heaven.

CHAPTER 17
OPERATION EXODUS

In August 1991, my friend, Frosty Fowler, a broadcaster from Seattle, Washington, and I were in Budapest, Hungary. We were there to see the facilities housing the Jewish immigrants who were waiting for planes to take them to Israel. We flew from Israel as guests of the Jewish Agency providing those facilities. We would then join Soviet Jews on a flight sponsored by Operation Exodus.

After spending two days at the "safe house" we went to the airport and boarded the airplane. We met one of the families, the mother, the father, the twelve-year-old son, and the baby daughter. They were one of many families that filled the plane that day, Soviet Jews going to Israel. I was actually participating in the beginning of the fulfillment of the vision God by His grace had given me in August 1974. I was overwhelmed!

The mother of this family was an English teacher and had taught her 12-year-old son English, so I was able to communicate with them. The father had been in Chernobyl during the meltdown of the nuclear reactor and was dreadfully ill. I was told about him by the

Jewish Agency before we boarded the airplane in Budapest. They informed me he was very, very ill. But the heart of the Jewish Agency was, "He is a Jew and he deserves the right to die in Israel, and we don't care what it costs us, or what the medical bills will be. We're taking him home to Israel."

In the Israeli army there is a rule. Never, ever do you leave a wounded soldier on a battlefield. Never! You have to go and get the injured soldier. We in the body of Christ should do the same. When we have a brother or sister who has had problems or who has fallen and been wounded in the battle, we need to rescue them. I know, because I have been rescued and restored.

God spoke this to Abraham, renewed it with Isaac, and again with Jacob, and said, "This is your land forever" (Genesis 15:18-19). God is a covenant keeping God. His covenants are everlasting. Deuteronomy 7:9 states, ". . . who keeps covenant and mercy for a thousand generations." I rejoice as I see God taking the Jewish people home to Israel. If He is keeping the covenant He made with Abraham, how much more is He going to keep the covenant He signed with the blood of His Son, Jesus? And, if He doesn't fulfill His word to the Jews, then how do we know He is going to fulfill His word to us?

"Who are these who fly like a cloud, and like doves to their roosts" (Isaiah 60:8)? Isaiah had never seen an airplane and he tried to describe Jews flying to Israel the best way he could. He prophesied, "to bring your sons from afar."

I became friends with this twelve-year-old boy. He was a wonderful child. He interpreted for me as we walked, up and down the aisle of the airplane, meeting people. I shall never forget as he turned to look at me and said, "Do you know what? I'm twelve, and next year I get to have my Bar-mitzvah in Israel." He also asked, "Who flew me to Israel?" Christians from forty nations had paid for that airplane going to Israel loaded with Soviet Jews. One thing that boy will never forget is that there are people called Christians who loved him and the Jewish Messiah with all their hearts, who helped to bring him home.

When we got to the immigration area at Ben Gurion Airport outside Tel Aviv, there was a little reception there. Then I had to go one way to passport control, and the Jewish family went the opposite direction to where Soviet Jews were being processed. I stood there with tears in my eyes, because in just the few short hours we had on the airplane, I had really become close to these people.

As I was drying my eyes, I remembered the first time I wept. Many years before, when I was a university student in Pullman, Washington, Jesus came and spoke to me. When I looked behind me to see who was talking, I couldn't see anyone. However, very clearly, the Lord Jesus began to reveal Himself to me. My life has never been the same since. I repented, received and accepted Him and He changed my life. That was in 1957.

As I was standing in that line with tears falling from my eyes, I felt two little arms wrap around my waist. The tears of that little twelve-year-old boy soaked through the back of my shirt. He stood there crying and holding me. I turned around, picked him up and hugged him. God is doing something. He is taking Jewish people home. He is doing this to ring a prophetic bell to say, "Get ready, Jesus the Messiah is coming!"

This flight actually began in the city of Jerusalem years before. In 1982, I was coming out of a building in Jerusalem when I heard someone yelling, "Steve! Steve!"

I looked up and down the sidewalk, and saw no one. As I began to walk again, the voice yelled again, "Steve, we're across the street."

That was how I met Gustav Scheller and his lovely wife, Elsa. Gustav explained that he had heard me speak in New Orleans years before. I didn't know him because we had never met. That soon changed. Our friendship would eventually help thousands of Soviet Jews go home to Israel.

This first meeting turned into dinner. Elsa was returning to their home in Bournemouth, England. So Judy and I invited Gustav to come and stay in our home in Jerusalem. He explained how the Lord had opened his heart for the Jewish people while he was in Southern Florida. Born in Switzerland, Gustav had been a businessman in England for about thirty years. He took a sabbatical to go to Bible School in Florida, and became very good friends with a Jewish couple from Jerusalem who were also students there.

The first morning Gustav came downstairs in our home, only one place was set at the table. He apologized for missing breakfast and said he would be very prompt from then on, "Just like a Swiss watch." I explained to him that we were not eating, but fasting. He joined us in the fast. Again, the next morning, only one place was set at the table. He asked how long we were going to fast, as he had never gone longer than one or two meals. Our reply was several days. Judy became quite concerned and made sure he had plenty of liquids. This was the beginning of a very precious relationship that would touch many lives.

Each day we would share from the Bible. I told him about the vision the Lord had given me in 1974 of the Soviet Jews' return to Israel.

He confirmed to me that I should write a book about this vision. The following year, 1983, I did write *EXODUS II, Let My People Go.*

Gustav invited me to Bournemouth, England, to share the vision and to speak about what God was doing with the Jewish people. That cassette literally went around the world.

In 1990, when Gustav and I began speaking about helping Soviet Jews fly to Israel, Operation Exodus was born.

One day, Gustav said, "Steven, airplanes are not enough. We need a ship."

I replied, "Wait a minute, not a ship. We need ships."

I told this to my dear brother and he said, "Why do you say 'ships'?"

I replied, "Because in the vision of 1974, when I saw the Jews come out of the Soviet Union, they boarded ships and went back to Israel."

Not only that, Isaiah 60:9 says, your sons from afar shall come by the ships of Tarshish and bring their gold and silver with them as they go back home to Israel.

Gustav replied, "Ships! Why did I ever meet you, Steven?"

He then said, "Let's begin with one."

I said, "Okay, let's begin with one ship."

In 1991 we began negotiations with officials in Israel and in the Soviet Union. You can't imagine what we went through. Gustav did most of the negotiating. Repeatedly, we were told it was an impossible task to start a shipping line to bring olim (new immigrants) to Israel.

Back in 1976, my friend John Osteen, a pastor from Lakewood, Texas, gave me a word. He said, "Steven, obey the slightest prompting of the Holy Spirit. When God tells you something, obey. Just do it, whatever it is. Just step out and obey God. If you don't have the finances, don't let that stop you from obeying. God will meet the need. If you are lacking in anything, in wisdom or any other thing, it is Jesus who is going to give you what you need, if you will step out and simply obey Him."

All we knew was to obey God. And as you obey God, He will open doors. The next thing we knew, we were in this office, and that office, in meetings with extremely high government officials.

I was flown by the Jewish Agency to Budapest, Hungary, to see what they go through to gather the Soviet Jews and to assess the logistical problems. It wasn't just a matter of putting some people on an airplane and flying them home.

The Agency didn't know where the people were coming from and when they would have enough people to fill the plane. So a safe house was needed to protect the Jewish people and their few belongings. They didn't know if they were coming by car, by taxi, or by train. Then, they had to be fed. Some of them were ill so they also had to have a doctor and a nurse. The logistical problems were immense.

Gustav and I would now be faced with the same problems. We started the "Exodus Shipping Line" to operate from Odessa, Ukraine, to Haifa, Israel. We were going to transport olim and their belongings. By airplane, they could only take with them 20 Kilos each, or roughly 44 pounds. By ship each person was allowed 250 kilos. We wanted to let them bring more, but the Ukrainian customs office set the limit.

After much time, money, and negotiations with the Soviet Union in Moscow, we received permission to begin shipping. This intensified the spiritual battle. Whenever you help Jewish people the battle gets much hotter. This brings you to your knees. After all, it is God's battle. Nehemiah 2:10 says, "When Sanballat the Horonite and Tobiah the Ammonite official heard of it, they were deeply disturbed that a man had come to seek the well-being of the children of Israel." Sometimes your faith is tested with fire.

In the midst of our celebration, the Soviet Union disintegrated right before our very eyes. The Ukrainians wouldn't honor our agreements with Moscow, as they were now their own republic. Gustav had to start the negotiations all over again. Talk about testing! But we pressed on in faith and prayer.

When I am told something is impossible, I believe it may be for man, but not for God. The Israeli side of the negotiations finally fell into place. Gustav and I were invited to the Kenesset (Israel's parliament) in Jerusalem. After meeting with the Chairman of the Immigration Committee, he arranged a meeting with another official. We began to wonder if we were running in circles, when this man said, "When can you have the first sailing?" He had the power to say yes or no, God had put us in the right place. Israel would provide their own teams of ship security. Israel would put 10 to 12 officials onboard to process the Soviet Jews while the ship was under way. And, Israel would control the food preparation under Jewish dietary laws. We agreed. Now all we had to do was find a ship.

Additionally, we had to find a safe house in Odessa for roughly 500 to 1,000 people. Have you ever taken a thousand people to breakfast? How about lunch or dinner? Some would have to be housed an entire week as a round trip would take one week. Security for the people and their belongings would also have to be provided. Indeed, God went before us and prepared the way. It was not easy because the enemy fought hard; however, all things fell into place.

Gustav and I went to Athens, Greece, to charter a ship from the harbor of Piraeus. After an intense meeting, we chartered the "Mediterranean Sky", a 515-foot ship with a crew, for three initial sailings.

We went from one or two crises a day to many. Each crisis could stop the ship from sailing.

On a Friday morning in December 1991, I flew from Israel to Athens with 12 volunteer intercessors, and 12 Israeli officials, eight security men and one rabbi. Rabbis in the government gave strict orders that the ship had to be under way before Shabbat (the Sabbath) began, which was sundown that day. If not, we had to wait until Saturday night, a delay of 24 hours. We needed to arrive on time in Odessa because the docking schedule at the pier in Odessa was set. If we missed our slot, no sailing.

One of the first things I did aboard the ship was to set up a 24-hour prayer chain, where at least two people would be in the prayer cabin at all times. Each volunteer was assigned a certain task. We had a doctor, a nurse, kindergarten teachers, a dirty diaper detail, people to instruct mothers about baby formula, Hebrew teachers, musicians, a secretary, a ship engineer, and laborers. Most importantly, they were intercessors.

We had a policy where if ever there was a crisis situation, no matter what anyone was doing, they dropped their task and immediately went to the prayer cabin. We saw the Lord end crisis after crisis as we pressed through in prayer.

As the sun began to set that Friday afternoon, the "Mediterranean Sky" sailed out of the harbor of Piraeus and as the Sabbath began, the Rabbi gave his blessing.

When we docked in Odessa, Gustav was waiting for us. His news caused us to pray even more. The customs officials were deliberately being slow in clearing the Jewish people to board. Gustav reported that all medicines, diapers, baby food, foreign currencies, gold, even wedding rings, were being confiscated. I went ashore and witnessed this for myself. In front of me, a customs official jerked a necklace with the Star of David from the neck of a young girl and said some anti-Semitic words to her.

This was the city whose gate I had prayed at for the Soviet Jews to be able to leave and go to Israel. It was bittersweet. I was at the bottom of the Potemkin Staircase where the four Smithskis had prayed in 1985. This time, the exodus was happening.

As our volunteers carried the hand luggage for the Jewish people and directed them to their cabins, fewer and fewer were boarding. The customs workers decided to stage a slowdown. Our contract with the port allowed only a specified amount of time at the dock. We were faced with having to pay excessive fees for any delays. We were due to sail at 6:00 p.m., the customs office closing time. However, we were able to negotiate a three-hour extension. At 9:00 p.m. there were still Jews that hadn't been cleared.

As we—Gustav, Shaul Zuella, Eliyahu Ben-Haim, myself, and the rest of the team—were praying the word of the Lord came from Ezekiel 39:28: "'. . . then they shall know that I am the LORD their God, who sent them into captivity among the nations, but also brought them back to their own land, and left none of them captive any longer.'"

We had our answer. We would not leave until every Jewish person in the customs hall was cleared. Gustav went to the port authorities and read this scripture to them. At the same time, one of the Israeli officials left the ship on a run. I don't know what transpired, but God moved, and the customs people kept working. At 11 minutes past midnight, the lines were cast off and we sailed out of Odessa with 476 Jewish immigrants making "aliyah". This was the first ship since 1948 to take Jewish refugees to Israel. On board were some very influential Israeli newspaper reporters to cover the story. This turned out to be very important, because while we were accused of "missionary activities" by the religious Jews in the government, the journalists published articles in favor of our project.

When we docked in Haifa, the news media and many government officials were there to meet us. I was taken immediately to port headquarters. I was then ushered into a private office and there was the man who had given us the authorization for the sailings. He was on the phone with one of the ministers of the Israeli Cabinet, a religious Jew. I could hear his screaming through the phone, but our "friend" said, "The ship will sail again." And that was that. Our "friend" told me he had spoken with his representative who was aboard the ship, the one who had run ashore when the Ukrainian customs workers staged their slowdown. The report was so favorable about us that the highest Israeli officials let us continue.

The problem for the religious Jews was that Christians were the ones bringing Jews to Israel, and that was not kosher to them, but it was to God. "Thus says the Lord God: 'Behold, I will lift My hand in an oath to the nations, and set up My standard for the peoples; they shall bring your sons in their arms, and your daughters shall be carried on their shoulders;'" (Isaiah 49:22).

After a few hours, we set sail a second time for Odessa with some new intercessors, a different security team, and Israeli immigration officials. Just before leaving Haifa, I talked with Gustav in Odessa and he asked whether I knew if any finances had come in for the second sailing. I replied, "No." When signing the ship charter agreement, we only had the money for the first sailing, and in five days the amount for the next sailing was due. In Philippians 4:6 the Apostle Paul said, . . . "let your requests be made known to God." So, on our knees again. I was on the ship and Gustav was in Odessa, and we couldn't have raised any money if we had wanted to. But God . . . !

On Saturday night, Peter, the owner of a shipping line in Seattle, Washington, was given a very vivid dream, and after waking his wife, she suggested he write it down. In the dream he saw refugees on a ship, and in a clear voice the Lord instructed him to help bring home the Lord's people. Peter didn't understand who or where the Lord's people were, he just knew he had to help them. Some hours later he called a prayer partner before going to church, explaining his dream. This man told Peter to look on the front page of the Sunday morning *Seattle Times* newspaper. On it were the refugees on our ship docking in Israel, the picture went around the world. Now he knew who, but what was he supposed to do? The Lord said in the dream, "Help." At church that morning, he shared this with a man who knew I was involved with the ship, so Peter sent a very large contribution to my wife, Judy, to help the "Lord's people to go home." This broke the dam holding back the finances, and money was then donated from over 40 nations. Jesus had done it again!

Again, we had delays in Odessa. Gustav informed me that he had received several faxes telling about daily debates taking place in the Kenesset about what we were doing, but the newspaper articles from the journalists who had been on the ship, kept the public informed of the truth.

We had crisis after crisis on the second trip as well. In one instance, a lady on board had set up shop in her cabin fortune telling. Kent, our doctor, informed me that many people were lined up outside her cabin door. Off we went to the prayer cabin. God hates witchcraft, it is an abomination to Him (Deuteronomy 18:9-14). We prayed that God would stop this woman. A short time after our prayer, we hit a storm that registered 10 on the Beaufort Scale (the highest being 12). Our 515-foot ship was tossed about like a cork. Green water was going over the ship's bridge, seven stories high. I went to the dining room and not one person was there. Even the crew was sick. I had to make my own meal. My parents had owned a boat since I was a young boy, and I like the water, the rougher the better. I went to the bridge to see the captain, but he was seasick too.

Needless to say, no more fortune telling went on during this trip. We never saw the woman again for the rest of that trip, even in calm waters.

In Haifa, I was given an ultimatum: either allow two groups of religious Jews to sail with us at no charge, or no third trip! They wanted to check on us to see if we were carrying on some kind of proselytizing. They would bring aboard their own Kosher food. I had to agree, and soon learned why Jesus called the religious Jews of His day, offspring of vipers (Matt. 12:34). I constantly had to ask Jesus for wisdom.

It was January 11, 1992, when we docked a third time in Odessa. I could write another book just about these three sailings. Customs officials were again stopping work. Not even half of the 550 Jewish people had been cleared to go aboard ship. It took nearly 36 hours longer to get them on the ship. The people couldn't leave the customs hall, and they had no food. When I shared this with the ship's captain, he asked if his cooks could prepare a hot meal for the waiting refugees. I said "yes, please do."

Our problem was, only those who chartered the ship and one other person could go ashore. That meant Gustav and me. I appointed Yehuda as the third. The cooks prepared the food and the three of us carried it into the hall and served the people. First we served the children. These Jewish people had come to Odessa from many areas of the former Soviet Union. They had been robbed, cheated, and mistreated. It was such a privilege to serve some of my people. Yehuda and I were asked to carry wedding rings, gold, and other valuables onto the ship, so the customs inspectors couldn't confiscate them. Isaiah 60:9 says, ". . . their silver and gold with them." Because we were not subject to a customs search, we loaded our pockets, went aboard, emptied them and went back again to refill them. Once aboard, we returned these items to the refugees.

Chaim, the leader of one of the groups of religious Jews, didn't like me at all. In fact, he became furious with me. His group refused to have anything to do with the other religious group aboard. They ate their food separately from each other and from us. And most of all, they wanted nothing to do with the olim, the new immigrants. Every day I would go out of my way to see Chaim and wish him a good day. He then confronted me and accused us of doing missionary activities.

I asked him, "Which activities? Was it picking up dirty diapers (which we supplied) three times a day from each mother's cabin? Was it teaching Ha Tikva, the Israeli National Anthem, or was it giving balloons to children who had never seen one before? What?"

His group of religious people didn't even lift one finger to help the refugees.

On the last night, when I authorized a banquet of roast beef and chicken, Chaim became extremely upset and began yelling and screaming at me. He and his select little group were eating the food they brought on board and forcing the olim to eat very bland food. I asked the ship's cooks to put on the grandest meal, with cake for dessert. What a happy and satisfied group of people we had aboard after that meal.

However, Chaim was so very angry. And I was bound to hear about this. He came to the table where I was sitting and demanded to know who authorized the change in menu.

I asked him, "Why, do you want some, too?"

I told him I would answer his question if he would answer mine.

"Chaim, who checked and gave permission for the food that is aboard this ship?" Several olim also gathered around us and they also asked, "Who?"

A rabbi on the first sailing was assigned to us to check out the food, and Chaim knew that.

His reply to me was, "Just a moment."

He went back to his group of a dozen religious Jews, they got in a huddle, and such shouting went on during their discussion. They could be heard throughout the dining room. I had to chuckle because I remembered the passage in Luke 20, when the chief priests, the scribes and the religious elders asked Jesus by what authority He did what He did. After many minutes, Chaim came back to me with his reply. If he said the other rabbi said the food was okay or kosher, then I could ask why he didn't he eat what was served to the olim. If he said the food was not good or kosher, then I could ask why he allowed it to be served.

He replied, "I don't know." He turned away, and that was the last time I spoke with him.

One thousand four hundred Jewish immigrants with many of their possessions were brought to Israel on the first three sailings. Gustav continued the sailings, and the 50th trip was completed in December 1996. The ship still continues on. Though I am no longer directly involved with the shipping, by 1998, twenty thousand will have been brought to Israel. The scriptures clearly say that the Gentiles have the responsibility of bringing the Jews to Israel in Isaiah 49, Isaiah 60, and in Romans 15:27.

CHAPTER 18

REDEMPTION

From the very beginning, the Lord has had a plan to redeem mankind to Himself. Genesis 12 contains God's plan of redemption. This plan includes what God is doing even today. Therefore, it is important to make sure we have a strong foundation in understanding God's redemptive plan in order to understand what God wants to do in end-time evangelism.

In Genesis 12 Abram demonstrated his faith in God. It was counted to him for righteousness and his name was changed to "Abraham". God breathed into him. When people reach a point where they realize they are sinners and in need of somebody to give them salvation, they can call upon the name of the Lord Jesus. After we each confess our sins, repent from them, and make Jesus Lord of our lives, it is then that God breathes His Spirit into us. The same thing happens to us that happened to Abraham. Then we are given new names, too. They are written in Heaven, new names (Revelation 2:17). The same thing was true for Sarah. Her name was changed from Sarai to Sarah.

"Now the Lord had said to Abram: "Get out of your country, from your kindred," (Genesis 12:1).

God's plan was to separate Abram from everything he was familiar with. From everything he had learned to depend upon.

God took him away from his surroundings and his father's house. God wanted Abram's dependence to be upon Him and Him alone. "To a land that I will show you." God had a place for Abram and you must also go to the place that He will show you. We need to follow in the footsteps of Abraham. "I will make you a great nation; I will bless you and make your name great; and you shall be a blessing." Abram had to be blessed before he could be a blessing. The same is true for us.

Then God said, "And in you all the families of the earth shall be blessed" (Genesis 12:3b). That is God's plan for salvation, evangelism, and harvest. It is all wrapped up in this very short sentence that He said to Abraham, "In you all families of the earth shall be blessed." God wanted what he had for Abraham for every single person who was on the face of this earth. God called Abraham to begin to fulfill the purpose that God had for him. Abraham was obedient.

Genesis 12:4: "So Abram departed as the Lord had spoken to him and Lot went with him. And Abram was seventy-five years old when he departed from Haran." He went to Canaan and when he arrived, there was a famine in the land. How did Abraham react? Abraham might have said something like this, "God, you didn't tell me there would be a famine in this land. All this great purpose you have for me . . . In me all the families of the whole earth are going to be blessed, and you take me to a place of famine? Lord, you didn't tell me about this." God doesn't tell us everything that is going to happen to us. Because if we knew everything that was ahead, we would not go.

The Lord has some good things planned for us and some not so good things, at least at first glance. We need God to effect a change in us so that we come to depend on Him and Him alone. So when the difficult times happen, He can guide us through them.

When arriving in Canaan and facing this great famine, Abraham continued on to Egypt and made a mess out of things; eventually he came back and never again left the land God promised to him.

God's plan is to bless the families of the earth through Abraham's seed. That is a great plan. In Genesis 22, God reconfirms His covenant with Abraham. This scripture tells us the story of when Abraham takes Isaac, his son, to the land of Moriah. The Angel of the Lord stops him from plunging the dagger into Isaac. Genesis 22:15-17 says, "Then the Angel of the LORD called to Abraham a second time out of heaven, and said: 'By Myself I have sworn, says the LORD, because you have done this thing, and have not withheld your son, your only son, in blessing I will bless you, and in multiplying I will multiply your descendants as the stars of the heaven and as the sand which is on the seashore; and your descendants shall possess the gate of their enemies'."

Jesus said, "I will build My church, and the gates of Hell shall not prevail against it" (Matthew 16:18). The reason Jesus was able to say this was because He had the promise that was made to the father of the faith. Abraham is the father of the faith of all those who believe (Romans 4:11). If you walk in faith, you are going to walk in the steps Abraham walked in. So you have some difficult times and some great times ahead. God said, "Your seed, Abraham, will possess the gate of their enemies." The gates of hell couldn't stop Jesus, nor will they stop you.

There are only two things God requires to reach every family in the nations. Genesis 22:18a states, "In your seed all the nations of the earth shall be blessed." Why? ". . . because you have obeyed My voice." The first is to obey God's voice. In Genesis 12, Abraham heard the voice of the Lord. He obeyed the voice of the Lord God.

I once had a crazy little business called "Dippy Duck Car Wash". Now for anyone who would name their business "Dippy Duck", God had better do something with him.

I had a sign thirty-seven feet high that had a reader board on it; you could read it from a great distance. One day a voice spoke to me and said,

"That is My sign."

And I said, "Yes, Lord. Amen. Hallelujah! One Jew to another, we'll do good business."

However, when the Lord told me what to put on that sign I said, "Dear God, no!"

But I obeyed. Jesus woke me up in the middle of every night and told me what to put on that sign from that day on. I had a tremendous longing in my heart. I wanted to know the voice of the Lord, but questions began to arise in me. Was this God speaking to me? Was it the Devil? Or was it just me? This was settled one day when the telephone rang.

I picked up the phone and said, "Dippy Duck Car Wash".

I heard a voice, and it said, "Hi."

And I replied, "Hi, Honey. How are you doing?"

It was my wife. Then the thought came to me, wait a minute. My wife didn't tell me who she was. She was a long distance away from me; all she said was "Hi." How did I know it was Judy's voice?

How did I get to know my wife's voice? I spent a lot of time with her. That's the secret. Can you imagine my wife calling me and saying, "Hi," and me asking, "Is this the Devil?" I began to realize: spend time with Jesus and you will know His voice. You can't always speak, often times you need to listen. Sometimes, a whole lot more listening than asking or speaking.

I would never know what God was going to do, but I had a steady stream of people coming to "Dippy Duck Car Wash" asking for prayer. Every day God gave me a prophetic message to put on the reader board. "Because you have obeyed My voice, I want to bless the families of the earth."

Abraham was a man who obeyed the voice of God. When Abraham died, God went to Isaac to reconfirm the covenant agreement He made with Abraham.

Genesis 26:2-5: "Then the LORD appeared to him and said: 'Do not go down to Egypt; dwell in the land of which I shall tell you. Sojourn in this land, and I will be with you and bless you; for to you and your descendants I give all these lands, and I will perform the oath which I swore to Abraham your father. And I will make your descendants multiply as the stars in heaven; I will give to your descendants all these lands; and in your seed all the nations of the earth shall be blessed; because Abraham obeyed My voice and kept My charge, My commandments, My statutes, and My laws.'"

Here we find the second requirement in God's plan of redemption. Keep My commandments. Abraham, number one, obeyed God's voice, and number two, kept His charge, His commandments, His statutes and His laws. Those were the two things required to bring redemption to the families of the whole earth. Obey God's voice and keep God's commandments. Two simple things—at least you would think they were simple. God's commandments are not grievous or burdensome (1 John 5:3).

God said to Jacob in Genesis 28:13-14: "And behold, the LORD stood above it and said: 'I am the LORD God of Abraham your father and the God of Isaac; the land on which you lie I will give to you and your descendants. Also your descendants shall be as the dust of the earth; you shall spread abroad to the west and the east, to the north and the south; and in you and in your seed all the families of the earth shall be blessed.'"

Again, God's ultimate purpose is to bring redemption to all people.

"Behold, I am with you and will keep you wherever you go and will bring you back to this land; for I will not leave you until I have done what I have spoken to you" (Genesis 28:15).

God spoke to Abraham and gave him His plan. He renewed it with Isaac and with Jacob, and then set out to do it.

God does things in a different way. Genesis 15:13: "Then He said to Abram: 'Know certainly that your descendants will be strangers in a land that is not theirs'." Here is a prophecy. Can you imagine? God has already told him, "Abraham, I'm going to bless you and I'm going to make you be a blessing. Through your seed, the families of the whole earth are going to be blessed. It's going to be incredible what I am going to do through you. And oh, by the way, they will be strangers in a land that is not theirs, and will serve there, and will be afflicted for 400 years."

"Oh, thanks, Lord!" I can just imagine Abraham saying.

God has a plan and God knows best. Sometimes we don't always see that until certain things have come to pass.

Genesis 15:14: "And also the nation whom they serve I will judge; afterward they shall come out with great possessions." Why are they going to come out with great possessions? God says, "I am going to send you and your people into 400 years of captivity down in Egypt. They're going to turn you into slaves, you're going to have a horrible time. But I will judge them, and when I judge them . . . I will then bring you out with great possessions. Why? Because I have a plan. I want to let every family on the face of the earth be blessed through you. I want my redemption to come to them and in order for it to spread, to get it out to the whole world, it is going to take a lot of finances. But I will supply it." A 400-year savings account.

God said you will come out with great substance, great abundance. They went to Egypt and the Egyptians gave them all their gold, silver, and treasures. They heaped it upon them. In fact, Moses called for an offering one day and pointed to the people and said, "Don't bring any more, we have enough" (Exodus 36:3-7). Wouldn't you just love to go to a meeting where somebody said they weren't taking an offering because they had plenty and didn't need any more?

Dear ones, that day is coming. The way money is raised by much of Christendom today is sometimes not through God. On that day, God will raise the finances. It won't be man trying to do it through some kind of system he has learned from others. Nor by the manipulation and misuse of scriptures. No, God will raise the finances.

Paul said in Philippians 4:6, get in your prayer closet and on your knees, "and make your requests known to God . . ."

Genesis 15:15-17: "'Now as for you, you shall go to your fathers in peace; you shall be buried at a good old age. But in the fourth generation they shall return here, for the iniquity of the Ammorites is not yet complete.' And it came to pass, when the sun went down and it was dark, that behold, there was a smoking oven and a burning torch that passed between those pieces."

Genesis 15:18 states: "On the same day the LORD made a covenant with Abram saying: 'To your descendants I have given this land'. . ." And He described that land. Who does the earth belong to? "The earth is the LORD'S and all its fullness, the world and those who dwell therein" (Psalm 24:1). It all belongs to God. Can God do with His property what He wants to? Of course, He is God. So He gave to Abraham and his descendants forever this little, tiny area of land we call Israel.

If you were to get in a car today and drive across Israel, it would take about two and a half hours at the widest spot. To drive the length of it, from Mount Hermon down to Eilat, would take maybe six and a half hours. But it's 5,700 years deep. Every crack, every rock, every hill, every valley is jam-packed with the history of this Book, the Bible.

God said, "You're going to go into exile, but I'm going to give you this land."

What is happening today? After almost 2,000 years the Jewish people have come back to the land that God promised them. Two thousand years out of the land and they came back speaking the language of their forefathers. Never before has this happened.

Many times you will meet people who are second generation in other nations who do not speak the language of their forefathers. Yet, after 2,000 years the Jews have come back speaking Hebrew, worshiping the God of their forefathers and keeping the feasts of their forefathers. People say, "Show me a miracle and I'll believe there is a God." Well, this is a miracle. Never has this happened for any other people.

In God's original plan of redemption, the two requirements for the Jewish people to carry it out were, "Obey My voice, and keep My commandments."

Four-hundred years had passed concerning the time God had spoken to Abraham. They had been in captivity as slaves, and they were then delivered by God through Moses.

Exodus 19:5: "'Now, therefore, if you will indeed obey My voice and keep My covenant, [there it is, the two things] then you shall be a special treasure to Me above all people; for all the earth is Mine. And you shall be to Me a kingdom of priests and a holy nation.' 'These are the words which you shall speak to the children of Israel.' So Moses came and called for the elders of the people and laid before them all these words which the LORD commanded him. Then all the people answered together and said, 'All that the LORD has spoken we will do.' So Moses brought back the words of the people to the Lord."

There we have it again. The two things. God told Moses to go back and tell the people to obey His voice. In John 10, Jesus said, "My sheep hear My voice." So Jesus is still saying the same thing that was said to Abraham, Moses, and the children of Israel. God also said, "You are going to be a kingdom of priests and a holy nation." Peter said that about those who are believers in Jesus in 1 Peter 2:9. We will be a peculiar people, a holy nation, a kingdom of priests and kings before the LORD.

All the children of Israel heard this from Moses and decided they would do exactly what God told them to do. They would listen to His voice, keep His commandments, be a holy nation, and be priests unto the Lord. Exodus 19:8a: "Then all the people answered together and said, 'All that the LORD has spoken we will do.'" God included the children of Israel to help bring redemption to all the families. His plan was unfurled and the Jewish people were to carry it out.

In Exodus 20:18: "Now all the people witnessed the thunderings, the lightning flashes, the sound of the trumpet, and the mountain smoking; and when the people saw it, they trembled and stood afar off. Then they said to Moses, 'You speak with us, we will hear; but let not God speak with us, lest we die.' And Moses said to the people, 'Do not fear for God has come to test you, and that His fear may be before you, so that you may not sin.' So the people stood afar off, but Moses drew near the thick darkness where God was." What were the two things God required? Number one, "Obey My voice." Moses was up on the mountain, God was speaking to him with thunder and lightning and the people became afraid and backed off saying, "Moses, we want to hear from you but don't let us hear the voice of God."

The first thing that God required them to do, which Abraham had done, Isaac and Jacob had done, that first requirement was now broken. Remember, they had just said, "We will do it."

However, when they saw the way God came and spoke, they didn't want to hear Him.

Exodus 32:1: "Now when the people saw that Moses delayed coming down from the mountain, the people gathered together to Aaron, and said to him, "Come, make us gods that shall go before us; for as for this Moses, the man who brought us up out of the land of Egypt, we do not know what has become of him." Aaron made the golden calf and broke the commandment of the Lord. The second requirement was now also broken.

Two things God required to bring His redemption: "Obey My voice and keep My commandments." And the Jewish people failed. What is it going to take to bring the redemption of God to all the various nations today?

I submit to you; it is going to take two basic things. Number one, obey the voice of the Lord. Number two, keep His commandments. Then you will see God reach out in a mighty way. If we don't, we will suffer in much the same way the children of Israel did. Remember when Moses came down from the mountain, in Exodus 32:25 it says, "Now when Moses saw that the people were unrestrained (for Aaron had not restrained them, to their shame among their enemies), then Moses stood in the entrance of the camp, and said, 'Whoever is on the Lord's side, let him come to me.' And all the sons of Levi gathered themselves together to him. And he said to them, 'Thus says the LORD God of Israel: 'Let every man put his sword on his side.'"

Why weren't their swords on their sides already? Where was Moses standing? He was standing at a gate with hundreds of thousands of people inside the camp, with no one to protect them from any enemy who would try to come in. Wouldn't you think, if you were standing guard at a gate, that you should have a weapon or weapons? They were naked to the extent that they had laid down their weapons. They got caught up in a great big party.

How often that happens in Christendom. They lay down their weapons and get caught up in a big party.

The children of Israel could not wait for the man of God to come down from the mountain. They couldn't wait upon the Lord, so what did they do? They made an idol. When God has something for you, don't move until you know it is He who has told you what to do. Because if you don't wait upon God, and move too quickly, you also could create an idol. It is a spiritual principle.

"'Let every man put his sword on his side, and go in and out from entrance to entrance throughout the camp, and let every man kill his brother, every man his companion, and every man his neighbor.' So the sons of Levi did according to the word of Moses. And about three thousand men of the people fell that day" (Exodus 32:27-28). This happened during the time of Shavout, the second great feast of the Jews. The New Testament calls it the Feast of Pentecost.

Moses came down from the mountain during Shavout. He found this terrible party going on, the people had laid down their weapons and made themselves naked. Then he asked, "Who is on the Lord's side?" The tribe of Levi came and Moses said, "Go and kill." So they went to the entrances of the camp and killed 3,000 people at the gates. Here God's plan of redemption was, that at another time, another Shavout, another Pentecost, the Holy Ghost would fall, and 3,000 wouldn't die. Instead, they would be filled with the Holy Spirit of God (Acts 2). They would turn the whole of Jerusalem upside down and begin to travel throughout the world with the Good News.

We shouldn't lose focus and lay down our weapons. There are many weapons in the Word of God. Why did they put them down? They would not wait on God, they didn't want to hear His voice, and they didn't want to keep His commandments.

The Jews failed. We must succeed. We are not going to fail because God's plan is still to bring forth His redemption through Abraham and through his seed. Who is the seed of Abraham? Galatians 3:26,27,29 also includes the Gentiles. "For you are all sons of God through faith in Christ Jesus. For as many of you as were baptized into Christ have put on Christ . . ."

And if you are Christ's. . ." verse 29. What does that mean? That means you are saved by faith plus nothing. You don't add to the salvation that God has given. ". . . then you are Abraham's seed, and heirs according to the promise." You become the heirs of the promise God made with Abraham, renewed with Isaac, and renewed with Jacob. You become heirs of the redemptive plan He had for the Jewish people. Obey

His voice and keep His commandments. God wants to use you in end-time evangelism in a way that we have never seen before. The whole world has never seen anything like what God is going to do. But He needs a people who will both hear and obey His voice and who will keep His commandments.

I can't think of anything more wonderful to do, than to cooperate with God in this plan that He started from the very beginning, and see it fulfilled in the last days. I have a desire in my heart to participate with God to accomplish His eternal plans and purposes.

You will be used by the Lord if you choose to cooperate with Him. If it is the desire of your heart to see His eternal purposes and plans accomplished, you will see the course of history and of nations changed.

When I was with the Kurds in northern Iraq, near the Turkish border, I just wept and cried. There were hundreds and hundreds of children following me. They surrounded me. I couldn't speak one word of Kurdish. But they were just all over me, I could have been the Pied Piper. I prayed, "What can be done here?" I knew we were only going to be there for an afternoon.

They were beautiful young people from about sixteen to seventeen years old, on down to little children. There was one young man who had on such a clean white shirt. That was amazing to see in that part of Iraq. He would stay way back, and I watched him out of the corner of my eye. Finally I trapped him, I sneaked up and tapped him on the shoulder; he just about freaked out. It turned out that he could speak a little bit of English. This was my only chance, so I just shared the

Gospel of Jesus Christ with him very simply, so he could share it with the others.

After I left Iraq, I began to meet many people the Lord had spoken to. He had put the Kurdish people on their hearts. Some had gone there and ministered to them. God's promise to bless the families is happening. I am just so thankful because I am playing a small part in that. God's eternal purposes and plans are going to be accomplished; you have to decide whether or not you are going to cooperate with Him in what He wants to do.

Operation Exodus II

CHAPTER 19

WHY IS GOD RETURNING THE JEWISH PEOPLE TO ISRAEL?

Lev Oshner was a hero of the Soviet Union in what the Soviets called "The Great Patriotic War" (World War II). He was a Colonel in the Russian Air Force. He was shot down three times and three times he returned to fly missions even though he had been wounded. He was made a "Hero of the Soviet Union". Many children throughout the USSR studied about this man because of his service to his country. He was a great role model.

One day, Lev realized that he didn't know the history and background of his people. He knew he was a Jew, but what did that mean? He obtained a Bible, which was difficult for him to get then, and began to read the scriptures. He realized that God had set aside a land called Israel for Jewish people, and that they would return to this land. He decided, "I want to return to Israel. I am a Jew, I want to go." He and his wife had decided to make "aliyah" (to go up) — to immigrate to Israel.

He joined with many other Jews and applied to leave the Soviet Union and immigrate to Israel. However, he was denied permission. He was called a "Refusenik". He was refused the right to return to Israel. However, he was in good company, because

Moses was the first Refusenik. Moses went to Pharaoh and said, "Let my people go!" Pharaoh refused. So Moses became the first Refusenik. Then through the plagues, God used Moses to deliver and lead the Jewish people out of Egypt.

Lev was refused the right to leave.

The authorities came to him and said, "Lev, listen. You are a 'Hero of the Soviet Union', the highest honor you can receive in the Soviet Union. ("Hero of the Soviet Union" twice, and they erected a monument for you.) You are studied by the school children. It is a very, very prestigious award to have. So many know about you. You can't leave the USSR and go to Israel. We'll give you an advancement in the Air Force, make you a general."

Lev said, "Here is your medal for 'Hero of the Soviet Union'. Here is my commission in your Air Force. Here is everything, I am going to Israel."

I met Lev in 1981. He had already been refused permission to go to Israel for sixteen years. I went to his very small apartment in the city of Minsk. At that time Minsk was the capital of Belorussian. Today it is called Bellarus. When I walked into Lev's apartment, his wife was lying on the couch. She was having a very difficult time breathing. She had a very serious heart condition and was taken out of the hospital and returned to their apartment.

The authorities told Lev, "You will see your wife die in front of your eyes, and the entire Jewish community is going to see it, because you have no rights and none of you are going anywhere. We want you to see her die. She will never receive any medical treatment again, ever."

When I went into their apartment, Lev was so thrilled to learn I was living in Israel. He was ecstatic, he began to plead with me to help him. He put a call out for other Refuseniks to join us. They crowded into the little apartment, into the bedroom and into the kitchen. We were wall-to-wall people, squeezed into this little place.

He said, "Steven, please, you have to do something. Go to President Reagan and plead my case, and get me released so I can go home to Israel."

I said, "I have no entrance into the Oval Office. I have no power to do that."

Lev replied, "Then go to the press of Europe and get my story spread throughout all the newspapers and the news media, because I want to go home to Israel."

I said, "I have no way to do that."

He said, "Well, you have to do something for me."

I replied, "I know Somebody more important and more powerful than President Reagan."

He said, "You do? Who is that?"

I said, "Get on your knees."

I will never forget that scene. Because of the number of people, we were very close together. I was nose-to-nose with Lev. I mean, I could feel his breath upon my face. I would carry this memory with me because it was then that I identified with Lev. I would never, ever forget this. Here was a man whose wife was dying and who longed to go home to Israel. And simply because they were Jews they were refused that right. I knew who was behind it. Mr. Brezhnev, who was the head of the Soviet Union at that time, was only a pawn. It was Satan who was behind the entire attempt to block and hinder them from going to Israel.

I prayed, "Lord, if You have ever given me a prayer, give me one now that would be like hitting a home run, and let it knock this couple right into Israel." After praying, I pointed my finger at his chest and said, "Lev, the next time I see you it will be in Jerusalem." That was it. Then we got up and went to synagogue. It was a very special time.

After that, in later years, I went back to try to see Lev, but he had moved. I found out his wife did die with no medical attention. The authorities wanted to make an example for the Jewish people to show that they weren't going anywhere. However, God's Word is settled forever in Heaven (Psalm 119:89). I never did get to see Lev again in the Soviet Union. I have never forgotten that experience. His breath—he'd just eaten garlic—was blowing on me. It was something that inspired me in intercession.

I knew the Lord would not leave the plight of the Soviet Jews as it was, such as it was with Lev.

Deuteronomy 30:1: "Now it shall come to pass, when all these things come upon you, the blessing and the curse which I have set before you, and you call them to mind among all the nations where the LORD your God drives you . . ." Here was a prophetic word to Moses. The Jews were going to be driven out of the land. They were going to go into a dispersion, the diaspora, to be scattered among the nations.

Deuteronomy 30:2-6: "and you return to the LORD your God and obey His voice, according to all that I command you today, you and your children, with all your heart and with all your soul, that the LORD your God will bring you back from captivity, and have compassion on you, and gather you again from all the nations where the LORD your God has scattered you. If any of you are driven out to the farthest parts under heaven, from there the LORD your God will gather you, and from there He will bring you. Then the LORD your God will bring you to the land which your fathers possessed, and you shall possess it. He will prosper you and multiply you more than your fathers. And the LORD your God will circumcise your heart and the heart of your descendants, to love the LORD your God with all your heart and with all your soul, that you may live."

Here a prophetic pattern was prophesied to Moses, there would be a dispersion and a return. They will be dispersed out of the land because of rebellion, but God says, "I will bring you back."

David also speaks about this in Psalm 53:6: "Oh, that the salvation of Israel would come out of Zion! When God brings back the captivity of His people, let Jacob rejoice and Israel be glad." The cry coming from David's heart is for the salvation of the Jews to come out of Zion. The Savior, Jesus the Messiah, certainly did. David is saying that salvation, a move of the Spirit of God in the hearts of the Jews, is going to happen and will be coming out of Zion. The psalmist says in Psalm 147:2, "The LORD builds up Jerusalem; He gathers together the outcasts of Israel." God's plan is to bring the Jews back to Israel, because He wants to give them salvation.

I'm the kind of person who begins to ask questions, like "Why, Lord? Okay, there is going to be dispersion. There is going to be a return. You are going to bring them back. You want to circumcise their hearts and the hearts of their descendants, so that they know You. That's wonderful, Lord, but why?" There is a purpose behind every single thing that God does. God never does things accidentally.

Jeremiah 23:3 says, "But I will gather the remnant of My flock out of all countries." ("ALL" countries.) ". . . where I have driven them, and bring them back to their folds; and they shall be fruitful and increase." In 1948, Israel was reestablished as a nation. The fruit of Israel is now filling the face of the earth (Isaiah 27:6). The people are increasing, they are growing in numbers. That was God's promise when He brought them back to the land. When did this begin? In 1948, right in front of our eyes. Today we are living in the hour that Jeremiah spoke about. We are seeing his prophecy come to pass.

Jeremiah 23:4: "'I will set up shepherds over them who will feed them; and they shall fear no more, nor be dismayed, nor shall they be lacking,' says the Lord."

This is the prayer I have for those who come back to the land. God promises to set up His shepherds. True shepherds who are filled with His Holy Spirit. They are going to pass on the heart of the Good Shepherd unto these people.

Then in Jeremiah 23:5-6, "'Behold, the days are coming' says the LORD, . . ." (This is prophecy, Jeremiah is talking about a future time.) ". . . 'that I will raise to David a Branch of righteousness; a King shall reign and prosper, and execute judgment and righteousness in the earth. In His days Judah will be saved, and Israel will dwell safely; now this is His name by which He will be called: THE LORD OUR RIGHTEOUSNESS.'"

God's plan is for redemption to come to all the families of the earth. The Jewish people failed; however, God never fails. God will keep His word to Abraham because that covenant is still in effect to this day.

God said He would raise up a righteous branch to come from the house of David, a King. However, to earn the right to come as a King and execute justice and judgment, He first had to come as a lamb led to the slaughter, taking on the sin of all mankind. The first time Jesus came, He did not come according to Jeremiah 23. No, He came according to Isaiah 53:7. He was the Lamb led to the slaughter. He laid down His life. Jeremiah records He is coming back as a King, executing justice and judgment.

Upon whom is He going to execute His justice and judgment? Is it only going to be on Israel? No! He is going to execute His justice and judgment on all the nations of the earth. Jeremiah is not referring to the first coming. This is the Second Coming of the Messiah.

One of the prophetic announcements of the Second Coming of the Lord is the return of the Jews from all nations. When He comes, Israel is going to dwell safely. Today Israel is not dwelling safely, so the prophecy has not been fulfilled yet. You can hardly open a newspaper or hear a news report in which something is not mentioned about the city of Jerusalem or Israel.

God says in Jeremiah 23:6, "In His days, Judah will be saved." I guarantee you, today Judah is not saved. All you have to do is go to Israel to understand this. There are many religious spirits and demons in Jerusalem. Jeremiah says demonic altars number as many as the streets (Jeremiah 11:13). People say, "Oh, the Holy City . . ." But, just try to go there to live. It is totally different to live in Jerusalem than to visit. But Jeremiah says, "Judah will be saved."

When is that going to happen? When the Lord takes them from all nations, and returns them back to the land. How is that return going to unfold?

Jeremiah 23:7 begins: "Therefore, . . ." The word "therefore" is a marker connecting what we just read to what we are going to read. "'Therefore, behold, the days are coming,' says the Lord, 'that they shall no longer say, 'As the Lord lives who brought up the children of Israel from the land of Egypt.'" One of the greatest feasts that Jewish people celebrate is "Passover". They are instructed by Moses to teach this to their children, to hand it down and to celebrate it every year (Deuteronomy 6).

The Passover. Coming out of Egypt. The plagues. A pillar of fire. A pillar of cloud. Crossing the Red Sea on dry ground. Pharaoh's army drowned. Water flowing from a rock. Manna from heaven. He says, "We're not even going to talk about it anymore?" Well, if I'm not going to talk about the exodus out of Egypt, what am I going to talk about?

We have the answer in Jeremiah 23:8a: " . . . but, 'As the Lord lives who brought up and led the descendants of the house of Israel from the north country' . . ." If you go due north from Jerusalem, you come to the Mediterranean Sea. I don't think there are many Jews there. When you go further north, you come to the city of Moscow. In the last days, from the north country God will begin to ring a prophetic bell. Wake up! Christians, God is ringing a prophetic bell! The bell is the return of the Jewish people from the north country back to their land, Israel. And it is the announcement of a return that is even greater. The return of the Messiah, Jesus, His second coming.

Verse 8 continues, "'. . . and from all countries where I had driven them.' And they shall dwell in their own land." The Lord showed this to me in Braunschweig in 1974. The book, *EXODUS II*, written in 1983, tells more of this.

This specific return is an announcement of the coming of the Messiah, Jesus. That's a gigantic, prophetic bell. Now we begin to understand why God is returning the Jews. It's prophetic, God has a plan, a purpose in bringing them back to Israel, to announce the coming of Jesus. Then He will execute justice and judgment on all the nations of the earth. Not just Israel.

Jeremiah 24:6-7: "For I will set My eyes on them for good, and I will bring them back to this land; I will build them and not pull them down, and I will plant them and not pluck them up. Then I will give them a heart to know Me, that I am the LORD; and they shall be My people, and I will be their God, for they shall return to Me with their whole heart." God unfolds His plan just as Moses said, as David penned and as Jeremiah spoke. First, God returns them to the land and then He will give them a heart to know Him.

The primary thing is that they must first come back to the land. That is a prophetic sign. A prophetic sign signaling the coming of the Messiah and that the Jews are going to come to salvation. God is doing it!

Jeremiah 31 is a chapter I encourage you to read and reread. It is vital in understanding the eternal purpose of God. It refers to the Jewish people, not Christians, not the church.

"'At the same time,' says the LORD, 'I will be the God of all the families of Israel, and they shall be My people.' Thus says the LORD: 'The people who survived the sword found grace in the wilderness—Israel, when I went to give him rest.' The LORD has appeared of old to me, saying: 'Yes, I have loved you with an everlasting love'" Without God's everlasting love for the Jewish people they would have been consumed a long time ago. "Therefore with lovingkindness I have drawn you. Again I will build you, and you shall be rebuilt, O virgin of Israel! You shall again be adorned with your tambourines, and shall go forth in the dances of those who rejoice. You shall yet plant vines on the mountains of Samaria; the planters shall plant and eat them as ordinary food. For there shall be a day when the watchman will cry on Mount Ephraim, 'Arise, and let us go up to Zion, to the LORD our God.' For thus says the LORD: 'Sing with gladness for Jacob.'"

Jacob. That's how you know this is not for the Christians, this is not for the church, this is for the natural Jew. It is for Jacob. Each time Jacob is written you cannot replace him with the church or with Christians. "Sing with gladness for Jacob. . ." (verse 7).

Who is supposed to sing with gladness for Jacob? Could it be you? "Thus says the LORD: 'Sing with gladness for Jacob, and shout among the chief of the nations; proclaim, give praise, and say, 'O LORD, save your people, the remnant of Israel!' (These are commandments.) Behold, I will bring them from the north country, and gather them from the ends of the earth, among them the blind and the lame, the woman with child and the one who labors with child, together; a great throng shall return there. They shall come with weeping, and with supplications I will lead them. I will cause them to walk by the rivers of waters, in a straight way in which they shall not stumble; for I am a Father to Israel, and Ephraim is My firstborn. Hear the word of the LORD, O nations, and declare it in the isles afar off, and say, 'He who scattered Israel will gather him, and keep him as a shepherd does his flock.' For the LORD has redeemed Jacob, and ransomed him from the hand of one stronger than he. Therefore they shall come and sing in the height of Zion."

You can go on and read the promises of the Lord. Who is going to proclaim these things? Who is going to pray these things? Who is going to praise these things? Who is going to sing these things? Dear ones, the redeemed of the Lord will. Jeremiah is saying, "Thus saith the Lord." It is now up to you to give back to the Jew. To show mercy back to them. In Romans 11:30-31 it says it is your duty to show mercy unto the Jew.

The Lord says, I'm going to bring them from the north country, and from the ends of the earth. It's God's plan. His remnant . . . He is bringing them back to the land.

(Again, the prophetic word.) Jeremiah 31:31: "Behold, the days are coming, says the LORD, when I will make a new covenant with the house of Israel and with the house of Judah—not according to the covenant that I made with their fathers in the day that I took them by the hand to bring them out of the land of Egypt, My covenant which they broke, though I was a husband to them, says the LORD. But this is the covenant that I will make with the house of Israel after those days, says the LORD: I will put My law in their minds, and write it on their hearts; and I will be their God, and they shall be My people. No more shall every man teach his neighbor, and every man his brother, saying, 'Know the Lord,' for they all shall know Me, from the least of them to the greatest of them, says the LORD. For I will forgive their iniquity, and their sin I will remember no more. Thus says the LORD, who gives the sun for a light by day, and the ordinances of the moon and the stars for a light by night, who disturbs the sea, and its waves roar (The LORD of hosts is His name): If those ordinances depart from before Me, says the LORD, then the seed of Israel shall also cease from being a nation from before Me forever."

The sun is still shining. The stars were out last night. The moon came out in His ordinances. And all that He has for Israel shall come to pass. He has not cast off Israel. When will He make the new covenant? When the Lord returns them to Israel because His love is everlasting toward them. We see a pattern. Return them to the land and then He will make a new covenant with them.

Chapter 32:37-42: "'Behold, I will gather them out of all countries where I have driven them in My anger, in My fury, and in great wrath; I will bring them back to this place, and I will cause them to dwell safely. They shall be My people, and I will be their God; then I will give them one heart and one way, that they may fear Me forever, for the good of them and their children after them. And I will make an everlasting covenant with them, that I will not turn away from doing them good; but I will put My fear in their hearts so that they will not depart from Me. Yes, I will rejoice over them to do them good, and I will assuredly plant them in this land, with all My heart and with all My soul.' For thus saith the LORD: 'Just as I have brought all this great calamity on this people, so I will bring on them all the good that I have promised them.'"

Here again we see the prophetic pattern. " . . . I will gather them from all the places I have scattered them, I will return them back to the land. . ." Remember the promise in Genesis chapter 15. God promised to give this land to Abraham and to his seed. That's it. It is settled. "When I bring you back to the land after the dispersion, then I'm going to make a new covenant with you."

We have a great assurance from the scriptures. Get them home. Because the largest and greatest move of the Holy Spirit upon Jewish hearts will happen when they are in Israel. "And so all Israel will be saved" (Romans 11:26).

Does that mean that we can stop sharing the gospel with Jews? No! Of course not (Romans 1:16). God's plan involves the participation and cooperation of His servants in spreading the good news of the death and resurrection of Jesus the Messiah. It is a mighty blessing and privilege to be messengers of His Word. Therefore it is imperative that Christians continue to not only pray for the salvation of the Jewish people, but also to share the gospel with them. In doing so, it is critical that Christians are aware of the traps and pitfalls that often hinder them in carrying out this work.

The enemy has very carefully poisoned our culture in a variety of ways, deceiving us and making us ineffective in the praise and obedience of our Lord Jesus Christ. A major way has been through the worldwide promotion of the ancient Greek culture. That is, Hellenistic philosophies, values, religion, art, sporting events (i.e. the Olympics), entertainment, etc. Remember, all Greek mythology and philosophy has its foundation in Nimrod's Babylon.

The entire theme of Hellenism is humanism. Humanism is basically the worship of man. This philosophy insists on "self", that is self-examination, self-fulfillment, self-love, and self will. Hellenism glorifies man, man's achievements, man's order, man's mind, and man's body (as evidenced in many sculptures). This way of thinking is the foundation for modern psychology. This inward focus has resulted in self-worship. And self-worship is the most prevalent form of idolatry today. So then, when Christians are influenced by this and even adopt Greek ways, not only are they guilty of the very same thing that Paul cited of the wayward Corinthians (1 Corinthians 1:10-25), but also the work of evangelism becomes perverted by self-will and self-accomplishment. People's own efforts and desires to measure their own success by the NUMBERS they seemingly lead to Christ clash with the will of God.

On the cross, did Jesus have a number of people by His side? Who was there to help Him? Not many. And yet consider, it was the greatest victory ever known. In His plan of evangelism to the Jewish people and the world, God will do the work and we must cooperate with him. God is longsuffering and He knows how to bring to pass the victory. That takes a burden off of me. I don't have to take every Jew from the Soviet Union, put them on my shoulder and swim to Israel with them. How could I do that with 2.7 million people? That would be a pretty tough job. I don't have to do that because God says He's going to do it. However, I must do what the Lord shows me to do.

I don't have any agenda or any empire to build. I say, "Lord, it's yours, You do it." My attitude was, "Jesus, follow me." The Lord had to teach me some things. The Lord showed me it is the responsibility of the Gentiles to help the Jews go to Israel (Isaiah 49:22-

23; Isaiah 60:8-11).

Consequently, God will bring the Jews back to Israel and make a new covenant with them.

We begin to understand more of God's plan. It was spoken to Abraham and He begins to carry it out. The prophecies are being fulfilled and we see them coming to pass this very day. Ezekiel 11:17: "Therefore say, 'Thus says the LORD God: I will gather you from the peoples, assemble you from the countries where you have been scattered, and I will give you the land of Israel.' "And they will go there, and they will take away all its detestable things and all its abominations from there."

When the kings of Israel came to power, some removed the idols out of the land, but they did not always remove those in the high places. (1 Kings 15:11-14; 1 Kings 22:43; 2 Kings 12:2-3; 2 Kings 14:3-4; 2 Kings 15:3-4, 34-35). God does not want idols to be left in the high places. Especially in Israel, which is His land. "The LORD loves the gates of Zion more than all the dwellings of Jacob" (Psalm 87:2).

Have you ever wondered why Jerusalem is still a city today, even though it has been totally and completely destroyed just under two dozen times? And yet all of the nations and all of the peoples that attacked Jerusalem and came against it are hardly even heard of today. And Jerusalem is built up, every single time. Why? Jerusalem is the only city mentioned in the Bible that God has chosen (2 Chronicles 6:6) and the only city placed in the midst of the nations (Ezekiel 5:5). Why? Because God set His name there.

Revelation 21 speaks of the New Jerusalem that will come down from heaven. I want to prepare for that day by studying the Jerusalem we have now.

God does not want demonic powers in the high places. Ultimately God has a plan to get the detestable and the demonic powers removed from the nation of Israel. He will give this responsibility to the Jews when He brings them back to the land (see Ezekiel 11:18).

I'm looking for that day. We have a lot of work to do, because there are still a lot of Jews around the world and God is going to bring them back. I'm looking for the day when Jesus is going to empower the Jews and they see to it that every detestable and demonic thing within the land of Israel is absolutely and totally destroyed, even from the high places. Could it be the idols and detestable things of other nations, will not be removed until the Jewish people do it in Israel?

In Ezekiel 11:19-20 we begin to see the second reason God is returning the Jews back to the land. "Then I will give them one heart, and I will put a new spirit within them, and take the stony heart out of their flesh, and give them a heart of flesh, that they may walk in My statutes and keep My judgments and do them; and they shall be My people, and I will be their God." Again, we see the pattern. Return them from the "diaspora" back to the land. It's another prophetic bell that God is ringing.

This is an announcement of the second coming of Messiah Jesus. When they come back they are going to take the detestable out of the way. Then the Lord is going to make a new covenant with the Jews, and He will give them a heart of flesh. No more stony hearts. If He can do it with the Jews, He can do it with all people.

During the spring of 1988, Judy and I led a tour group to Israel to celebrate Israel's 40th anniversary as a nation.

In the lobby of the hotel where our group was staying, as I conversed with friends, someone ran up behind me, grabbed me, spun me around, and kissed me right on the lips. Because that's the way men greet one another there in the USSR, I knew he had to have come from there.

I was quite surprised when this happened. But when I saw who it was, my eyes filled with tears of joy. It was Lev. Lev from Minsk! I never saw him again in the Soviet Union, but here he was, in Jerusalem.

He said to me, "Steven, President Reagan did not bring me home to Israel. The press of Europe did not bring me home to Israel. The Lord God of Israel brought me home!"

Lev then began to repeat word for word the prayer that was said when we were nose to nose, with his breath blowing on me, years before.

"I was brought home on a prayer to my God," he said.

Whew!

CHAPTER 20
HALLOWED BE YOUR NAME

"How beautiful upon the mountains are the feet of him who brings good news, who proclaims peace, who brings glad tidings of good things, who proclaims salvation, who says to Zion, 'Your God reigns!' Your watchmen shall lift up their voices, with their voices they shall sing together; for they shall see eye to eye when the LORD brings back Zion. Break forth into joy, sing together, you waste places of Jerusalem! For the LORD has comforted His people, He has redeemed Jerusalem. The LORD has made bare His holy arm in the eyes of all the nations; and all the ends of the earth shall see the salvation of our God" (Isaiah 52:7-10).

It makes no difference if your feet look bony, skinny, fat, short or long, they are beautiful to the Lord if you are proclaiming the gospel, peace, bringing glad tidings and proclaiming salvation. Those who do will see the Lord bring back Zion, comfort His Jewish people, and redeem Jerusalem. This will be done in the eyes of all nations, and the salvation of God will go to the ends of the earth.

Israel is a key to end-time evangelism. Notice it is, "a key", not "the key". The end-time harvest is very closely associated with the return of the Jewish people to Israel, and it will be the greatest evangelistic move of God ever.

Does that mean evangelism will not take place in the meantime? Of course not. People are giving their lives to Jesus worldwide. However, get ready; it will increase beyond anything we have ever seen up to this point.

One day after Jesus had prayed in a certain place, one of His disciples witnessed Jesus' pattern of prayer and His relationship with His heavenly Father. It must have been quite different from what he saw in the lives of others. He was so moved by observing Jesus, he asked Him a question. He did not ask, "Lord, teach us to preach." Nor, "Lord, teach us to play." But he asked, "Lord teach us to pray."

"So He said to them, 'When you pray, say: Our Father in heaven, hallowed be Your name'" (Luke 11:2).

How is our Father's name hallowed? How is His name honored, made holy, sacred, whole and complete? One of the ways the name of our heavenly Father will be hallowed is going to be when He takes the Jewish people out of the lands they are in, and returns them home to Israel. God will be hallowed in the sight of the Gentiles as He removes the Jewish people.

"I will accept you as a sweet aroma when I bring you out from the peoples and gather you out of the countries where you have been scattered; and I will be hallowed in you before the Gentiles. Then you shall know that I am the LORD, when I bring you into the land of Israel, into the country for which I lifted My hand in an oath to give to your fathers" (Ezekiel 20:41-42).

In 1991, the Iron Curtain began to come down. The place the Iron Curtain was first penetrated was at the Hungarian-Austrian border. I was in Budapest attending a national prayer conference when this happened. When we entered, our team had to go through customs controls at the border before the conference began. We also had to have visas. It took us about half a day to get into Hungary. But when we came out, nothing! Nothing! We drove right through the border. It was unbelievable! It had been absolutely cracked, torn down. No customs or border controls. The east Europeans were wild with enthusiasm.

I rejoiced because when I saw the Jews coming out of the Soviet Union in the vision of August 1974, there was no Iron Curtain, no Berlin Wall. None of that was there. They came right on out. Nobody stopped them. I remember a prophetic word from 1975 that went something like this. "There is no gun, tank, bullet, or missile that the enemy has that is strong enough, including an Iron Curtain, that can stop the Holy Spirit of God from penetrating the heart of a person who is open to receive Him."

Today, that Iron Curtain is not there. Sadly, in spite of this, there is a curtain, a hardness, that can come around the heart of a man stopping the Spirit of God from entering. We need to be humble as David was, and ask God to search us. "Search me, O God, and know my heart; try me, and know my anxieties; and see if there is any wicked way in me, and lead me in the way everlasting" (Psalm 139:23-24).

As the Iron Curtain came down something began to occur. People began to take the gospel into the former Soviet Union in an unprecedented way. Millions and millions of Bibles were taken in. There was a Bible School in Sweden whose students took a train through Russia. They started in St. Petersburg and went all the way across to Siberia. It took them six weeks to make that journey. They stopped along the way and were able to preach the gospel in each place they stopped. They handed out medicines, food, clothing, and Bibles.

What was happening? This was the Soviet Union. Every time I went to the USSR, the first question asked of me prior to 1991 was, "Do you have any Bibles?" One time, I finally got bold enough to question a customs man in Khabarovsk, Far East Russia. (Being far away from Moscow, I felt safe asking. It was eleven time zones away. The Soviet Union was the largest country on the face of the earth. It comprised one-sixth of the earth's land mass. Russia still is the largest country.)

I said, "May I ask you a question?"

He replied, "What is it?"

I asked him, "Why are you so concerned about a book that is written about a God that you people claim does not exist?"

He looked at me dead serious as he said, "Because we're not so sure."

Now millions and millions of Bibles are being taken into the former USSR. Evangelistic campaigns all across the nation. Army bases open to evangelism. Every school of the former Soviet Union is open for people to go and preach the gospel and pray.

What is happening? God said, "My Name will be hallowed in the eyes of the Gentiles when I take the Jews out of a country." The gospel can now be preached. end-time evangelism is exploding, and there is a harvest the likes of which they have never known.

Multitudes of people have come to know Jesus in the former Soviet Union. I submit to you that none of this started, to this extent, until 1991 when the Iron Curtain came down and the laws were changed allowing the Jews to immigrate to Israel. God said through the prophet Ezekiel thousands of years ago, "I will be hallowed in you when you leave a country, and I will bring you to Israel."

I began to see the relationship between the exodus of Jews to Israel and great evangelistic harvest while in Birmingham, England. When I was there, I shared with about seventy pastors. They asked me to speak about Israel and end-time evangelism. God began to speak to my heart and opened up the scriptures, and I began to see more of God's plan. I saw that the Lord has a mighty, mighty move of His Spirit for end-time harvest that is triggered when His ancient people are taken back home to their land. Remember, Jeremiah 31 says, ". . . you proclaim, you praise, you sing, you dance, you speak about this." We get to cooperate with God.

If God does not keep His word with the Jew, what hope, what foundation, what evidence do you have that He is going to keep His word with you? You have absolutely no hope if God fails Israel. See what God is doing and rejoice. Since 1991, over 900,000 Soviet Jews have gone to Israel. It was almost impossible for them to go prior to then.

There is incredible evangelism going on in the Soviet Union. However, take a look at America. Isn't it interesting? No prayer in schools. Today, you cannot do in America what you can do in Russia with the gospel. Try to have a Christmas manger scene in a city square. Or let a mayor try to proclaim a "Prayer Week". No, you will find the ACLU, lawyers, this people and that people, and they will have you in court. There is an absolute clamp down happening in America with respect to the gospel. Cities are passing all kinds of laws concerning what they call "Mega Churches". In the city where I live, you cannot build a church to house more than 1,000 people. You cannot get a building permit. Can you imagine? In the United States of America? A total, complete block. It is now called separation of church and state.

Before 1990, I had to do things underground in the Soviet Union. Today, everything is open. Why? Because the Lord began to do what Jeremiah, Ezekiel, Moses, and David said He would do. He is returning His people back to Israel. He is being hallowed in their eyes.

We are living in that day and age. This could never have happened in former generations. It could not have happened before 1948. Israel was not a nation then, but now is. In His Word, God tells us the reasons for what He is doing.

Ezekiel 36:19-23: "So I scattered them among the nations, and they were dispersed throughout the countries; I judged them according to their ways and their deeds. When they came to the nations, wherever they went, they profaned my Holy Name—when they said of them, 'These are the people of the LORD, and yet they have gone out of His land.' But I had concern for My Holy Name, which the house of Israel had profaned among the nations wherever they went. Therefore, say to the house of Israel, 'Thus says the LORD God: I do not do this for your sake, O house of Israel, but for My Holy name's sake, which you have profaned among the nations wherever you went. And I will sanctify My great name, which has been profaned among the nations, which you have profaned in their midst; and the nations shall know that I am the LORD,' says the LORD God, 'when I am hallowed in you before their eyes.'"

All the nations will know who the Lord is; He is doing it for His Holy name's sake. Again it is stated He will be hallowed in the Jewish people before the eyes of the Gentiles.

He won't do this for the sake of the Jews; they don't deserve it. The Jews don't deserve anything. But the Gentiles don't deserve anything either. None of us deserve anything. It is because of God's mercy and His grace that we receive anything. The Lord entered into a covenant with Abraham. He made a promise and is going to fulfill that promise. There would be a dispersion, but there would also be an ingathering.

The former Soviet Union is having, at least for a period of time, a harvest of souls. However, we haven't seen anything until the Jews of America go home to Israel. There are about six million Jews in North America. The largest concentration of Jews in one city is not in Jerusalem nor in Tel Aviv. It is not even in Israel. It is in Brooklyn, New York, where there are about two million Jews. There are more Jewish people in the United States than in Israel. This will change.

God said, ". . . all countries I have driven them to will return." Praise the Lord! I want to be part of it. I want to be part of the end-time evangelism. I want to be a part of the end-time harvest. I want to be a co-worker with the Lord in what He is doing. But I also submit to you the fullness of end-time evangelism in the United States and Canada will not happen until the Jews of North America begin to return to Israel in large numbers. And not just from America, but from all countries.

Why will the evangelism be so great in the United States? Because there are so many Jews in America. The harvest will be far greater than in Russia or in any other nation.

What is it going to take to get the Jews out of America, "the land of the free and home of the brave"? It is going to be cataclysmic. Look at what the Soviet Union has gone through. It is not even a nation anymore. God has a plan for North America. God is going to hallow Himself in the Jews of North America before the eyes of all the people of the United States and Canada when the Jews go back, just as for the other nations. Will it be economic collapse that will cause it? Probably a part of it. However, the cataclysmic events will happen and the Jews will then say, "We've got to go to Israel." There will be no place of safety for them apart from the land God said was theirs forever. Why? Because God's plan is to deal with their hearts when they get to Israel.

Continuing in Ezekiel 36:24-28: "For I will take you from among the nations, gather you out of all countries, and bring you into your own land. Then I will sprinkle clean water on you, and you shall be clean; I will cleanse you from all your filthiness and from all of your idols. I will give you a new heart and put a new spirit within you; I will take the heart of stone out of your flesh and give you a heart of flesh. I will put My Spirit within you and cause you to walk in My statutes, and you will keep My judgments and do them. Then you shall dwell in the land that I gave to your fathers; you shall be My people, and I will be your God."

The Lord is going to bring salvation to His ancient people through a new covenant. As they leave the nations they are in, He is also going to bring salvation unto the people they leave. Unprecedented moves of evangelism and harvest will occur, the likes of which we have never seen in the history of all mankind. God determined to do this at a certain time in our history, and I believe this is that time. Isn't that just absolutely exciting?

Oh Lord, where are the intercessors? There are some. I have seen some and I have met some. Lord, give believers a burden for what you are doing, for their nations and their continents. When the Jews leave and go home to Israel, look for the end-time harvest. At this time God is looking for those to stand with Him in prayer and in readiness to help Jewish people return to

Israel. You are going to be at the right place at the right time. However, you need to count the cost. Helping the Jews return to Israel has never been the most popular thing to do. Rahab did, even at the threat of her own life (Joshua 2). As a result, her whole family was saved because she helped two Jews (Joshua 6).

All the nations will be involved in this great end-time harvest. God has put a burden on my heart concerning the Jews in the United States. The burden I had when I went to Jewish communities in Russia, beginning in 1975, to tell them God had prepared the way for them to go to Israel, I now have for other nations. As God opens doors, I plan to go to Jewish communities in the United States and other countries, to tell them to prepare to go to Israel. Others are doing this already, and I will too.

I remember the problems I had in the Soviet Union. I was followed by the KGB. I was kicked out of homes because people thought I was coming to cause political problems or trouble. Some Jews did not want to hear, and because of their pride neither did some Christians. But many did hear. However, I know when the Lord sends me, He will be with me. Because He has a plan. He has an eternal purpose that He is going to bring to pass. As the seed of Abraham, we will be a blessing to the families of the whole earth. God is hallowed in the Jews as they return to Israel. And when they return and receive their salvation, God is going to let salvation come in an incredible way to the nations they leave.

Does every Jew have to go back to Israel?

Ezekiel 39:25-29 says, "Therefore thus says the LORD God: 'Now I will bring back the captives of Jacob, and have mercy on the whole house of Israel; and I will be jealous for My holy name —after they have borne their shame, and all their unfaithfulness in which they were unfaithful to Me, when they dwelt safely in their own land and no one made them afraid. When I have brought them back from the peoples and gathered them out of their enemies' lands, and I am hallowed in them in the sight of many nations, then they shall know that I am the Lord their God, who sent them into captivity among the nations, but also brought them back to their own land, and left none of them captive any longer. And I will not hide My face from them anymore; for I shall have poured out My Spirit on the house of Israel,' says the LORD God."

He will leave NONE of them among the nations; ALL will be returned to Israel.

There is a great hope for America. There is a great hope for the nations. And the hope I am writing about, is the hope of salvation coming to multitudes of people. As we see God keeping His word to the Jew, how much more can we all rejoice in the covenant that He made with us and signed with the blood of His Son, Jesus? It's going to be unprecedented. His Name will be hallowed even as Jesus taught His disciples to pray.

Let's just say it:

"Our Father who art in Heaven, hallowed be Thy Name. Thy kingdom come, Thy will be done on earth as it is Heaven."

Father, I pray that Your heart has been communicated in this, the hope for the nations and the hope for the children of Israel. Let Your name be hallowed. Lord, You are doing this for Your holy name's sake. I thank You, O God, that You allowed us to be alive at this time to cooperate with You in what You are doing in these last days. Lord, You want harvest to come to the nations. My God, let us be there to be instruments of righteousness in Your hand, to share the gospel. That multitudes and multitudes of people would know who You are and receive You. Jesus, we look for Your coming. Seal this, Father, in the name of Jesus.

A Summary Of Why God Is Returning
The Jewish People To Israel

1. It is God's promise.
Deut. 30:1-6; Psalm 53:6,147:2;
Isa. 11:11; Isa. 43:5-6;
Jer. 16:14-15, 23:3-8, 24:6, 30:3, 31:8, 32:37
Ez. 11:17, 20:41, 28:25, 36:24, 39:25;
Zeph. 3:20

2. To announce the second coming of the Messiah.
Jer. 23:5-6

3. To make a new covenant with the Jewish people.
Jer. 24:7, 31:31-33, 32:40; Ez. 11:19, 36:25-27

4. To remove detestable abominations from Israel.
Ez. 11:17-18

5. The name of the LORD is hallowed.
Ez. 20:41, 28:25, 36:23, 39:27

6. Evangelism.
Ez. 36:23

7. To sanctify the name of the LORD.
Ez. 36:23

CHAPTER 21
WHAT CAN I DO?

I am often contacted and asked, "What can I do? How can I help? What can my part be in this?"

These questions generally arise when prophetic scriptures are revealed. It happens to me. We are not supposed to just sit around and twiddle our thumbs and say, "Oh, that's nice." God wants us to join Him in seeing the scriptures fulfilled.

"For the eyes of the Lord run to and fro throughout the whole earth, to show Himself strong on behalf of those whose heart is loyal to Him" (2 Chronicles 16:9). What father doesn't enjoy having his children doing things with him? So it is with our Heavenly Father. He longs to have an intimate relationship with us and work together with us.

If these questions arise in you, first I suggest you investigate in the Bible for yourself to see if these things are true. Pray and ask the Lord what He would have you do. God will confirm what He tells you. Then obey.

The most important thing needed is prayer. Usually when I say this, many ask, "Yes, but what can I

DO?" Prayer is the most important action that can be taken after the prophetic scriptures are known. Daniel 9 is a classic example of this. What did Daniel do after he understood the prophetic scriptures? He prayed, he repented, he prayed, and prayed again. It is so important to pray; it is something great. I cannot stress this enough. The prophetic journeys described in this book only lasted days, but up to three years of prayer went into each trip.

Intercession is the highest calling. In the Holy Place inside the tabernacle that God gave to Moses, the Ark of Testimony was a cubit and a half high (Exodus 25:10). The table for the shewbread was also a cubit and a half high (Exodus 25:23). But the altar of incense was two cubits high. The highest altar was the one representing intercession (Exodus 30:2). The highest ministry of Jesus today is, "He ever lives to make intercession for them" (Hebrews 7:25b). This is first and foremost.

One type of person God seeks after is an intercessor (Ezekiel 22:30). If you want God to seek you, intercede. He will be there.

Prayer had to go on for years and is still needed for the Jewish people in the former Soviet Union as they make their aliyah to Israel.

There are also practical ways to help.

When the Jewish people return to Israel from North America and other parts of the world, will you help them? This is a question that needs to be settled in your heart now.

As I mentioned before, Rahab in Joshua 2 hid and helped two Jewish spies escape from Jericho so they could return to their people—at the threat of her life—would you do the same? She and her whole family were the only ones saved when Jericho was destroyed (Joshua 6:22-25).

In Ruth 1:16-17, we have the covenant of the Moabite woman Ruth with Naomi, a Jewess. As a result, Ruth later marries Boaz and becomes the great-grandmother of David, the great King of Israel. From this lineage came the Messiah! "I will bless those who bless you" is still in effect today.

Some people ask, "Why should I help the Jews? They are rich and have big businesses." It is because we will see dramatic changes and the Jewish people will need help to get to Israel. God will test believers to see if their hearts concerning the Jews are in accordance with His heart toward them (Isaiah 40:1-2; Romans 15:27; Romans 11:17-27).

It is very interesting to me that I am meeting people in North America who are making preparations to help the Jewish people, just as I met those in the 70s and 80s in Europe getting ready to help the Soviet Jews.

For example, in October of 1997 I met a native American Indian man. He told me he was spreading the word among his people to prepare themselves to help Jewish people go to Israel. Not only that, we were introduced to one another by a person who had the same burden.

This time, in North America, God is again orchestrating believers to help the Jews. I would not be at all surprised to find He is speaking to Christians on other continents as well. It is exciting to hear from the Lord, but it will take perseverance to carry out the Lord's plan.

Some people will want to help financially, and this is also very important. Presently, it costs about $350 to $400 USD to help one Jewish person in the former USSR to go to Israel. You can see that it is very costly for a family, and most have nothing. Maybe you, your family, prayer group or church would like to sponsor one or more Jewish people to go to Israel.

In any case, the Father's plan includes the direct involvement of His children. We need to be intercessors and live in obedience to His commands, looking to the scriptures to understand His prophetic plan.

Operation Exodus II

Operation Exodus II

CHAPTER 22
WHAT IF I DON'T?

I have been asked through the years if there are consequences for the Gentiles if they do not stand with the Jewish people.

A principle we have learned about intercession was that we pray "for" something, before praying "against" it. Using this principle, consider this.

The Lord spoke to Abraham in Genesis 12:3, "I will bless those who bless you . . ." This word is still in effect today. Notice it is plural and positive, "those, bless." This is God's desire, that many would bless the Jewish people, so He in turn can bless them. The Hebrew word "bless" here is, "barak". It means to kneel down, congratulate, bless, praise, to speak well of, salute, thank. Toward God, it is an act of reverence and worship. Toward man it is a benefit, to receive abundantly. Deuteronomy 33 contains the blessings given to the tribes of Israel. Verse 3 states, "Yes, He loves the people; all His saints are in Your hand; they sit down at Your feet; everyone receives Your words."

Then come the blessings. Let's look at what three tribes received.

"And of Joseph he said: "Blessed of the LORD is his land, with the precious things of heaven, with the dew, and the deep lying beneath, with the precious fruits of the sun, with the precious produce of the months, with the best things of the ancient mountains, with the precious things of the everlasting hills, with the precious things of the earth and its fullness, and the favor of Him who dwelt in the bush. Let the blessing come 'on the head of Joseph, and on the crown of the head of him who was separate from his brothers.' His glory is like a firstborn bull, and his horns are like the horns of the wild ox; together with them He shall push the peoples to the ends of the earth; they are the ten thousands of Ephraim, and they are the thousands of Manasseh" (Deuteronomy 33:13-17).

Along with this blessing comes responsibility. Romans 15:25-27 shows this plainly. "But now I am going to Jerusalem to minister to the saints. For it pleased those from Macedonia and Achaia to make a certain contribution to the poor among the saints who were in Jerusalem." (Paul is bringing to Jerusalem offerings collected by Gentiles.) "It pleased them indeed, and they are their debtors. For if the Gentiles have been partakers of their spiritual things, their duty is also to minister to them in material things."

This could not be stated any more clearly. The Gentiles who receive the Jewish Messiah, Yeshua (Jesus), have a duty to minister to the Jewish people with material things. If you have come into the Jews' spiritual blessing, you have a responsibility back to them. The prophets were Jewish. The Bible is a Jewish book. The writers of it are Jewish. The covenants were made with the Jews. The Messiah is a Jew. The first church was 100% Jewish. Jesus said, ". . . For salvation is of the Jews" (John 4:22). If it were not for the Jewish people you would not have any of these, and where would you be?

Have you received any of these spiritual blessings? If so, it is now your duty to show mercy to the Jewish people and bless them. The church and Christians who are without pride will do this. Pride blinds us from the truth.

Suppose, however, someone chooses not to bless the Jewish people. Are there consequences?

Again, in Genesis 12:3, it is stated by God Himself, ". . . I will curse him who curses you." This also is in effect to this day. The covenant Jesus fulfilled was the covenant of the "law" given to Moses, not the covenant with Abraham. The Abrahamic covenant is in force today as much as the day God made it.

Notice this statement is in the singular and negative, "him, curse." God wants us to understand His ways as Moses did (Psalm 103:7).

Ultimately, the Jews have one enemy, Satan. The problem is that Satan has deceived so many, even Christians. Take for instance, replacement theology. Replacement theology teaches that the Jewish people had their opportunity to accept their Messiah; instead they rejected Him. Consequently, God is finished with the Jews and Israel. The Jews are now replaced by the Christians, and Israel is now replaced by the Church.

Nothing could be further from the truth. To begin with, Genesis 12, Jeremiah 31, Romans 9, 10, 11, and other chapters would have to be removed from the Bible.

To these people, the reestablishment of Israel as a nation in 1948 was a freak accident of history. I read a so-called "Christian book" which stated, "A Christian would be better off going to Timbuktu than ever going to Jerusalem."

Romans chapter 11 is very clear in stating not all Jews were broken off the olive tree. "And if some (not all) of the branches were broken off, and you, being a wild olive tree, were grafted in among them, and with them became a partaker of the root and fatness of the olive tree, do not boast against the branches" (Rom. 11:17-18), ". . . Otherwise you also will be cut off" (Romans 11:22b).

The basis of Paul's statement here is found in Genesis 12:3. The word "curse" is used two times in English, but not in Hebrew; they are two separate words.

The first time the word "curse" is used, it says God will curse. The Hebrew word is "qalal". It means to bring harm or trouble, to execrate, to denounce scathingly, to loathe, to abhor. God will bring harm and trouble to those who curse the Jew.

The second use of the word "curse" is a different Hebrew word; it is "arar". It means to make light of or to treat lightly, to despise, to esteem slightly, to revile, show contempt, trifling, to ridicule. Those who curse the Jewish people in these ways have an enemy, the LORD GOD OF ISRAEL.

If you have cursed the Jewish people by despising them, ridiculing them, or treating them lightly, ask God for forgiveness. Otherwise, He is your enemy.

If you are involved in replacement theology, REPENT. God will forgive you. Do not take this lightly.

Zechariah 12 states the consequence for nations that do not stand with the Jewish people. God uses the city of Jerusalem as a measure of blessing and cursing. "Behold, I will make Jerusalem a cup of drunkenness to all the surrounding peoples, when they lay siege against Judah and Jerusalem" (Zechariah 12:2).

The world refers to what the Bible calls Judah and Samaria as "the West Bank". Today, as the conflict between Israel and the Palestinian Liberation Organization (PLO) has progressed, each side fighting for more of the land God promised Abraham, many nations have decided to take sides. And many have come against Israel's claim. I have deep concern for those nations because of the terrible consequences that God has promised to those who would side against Israel. The Word tells us that they are in big trouble.

"And it shall happen in that day that I will make Jerusalem a very heavy stone for all peoples; all who would heave it away will surely be cut in pieces, though all nations of the earth are gathered against it" (Zechariah 12:3).

"It shall be in that day that I will seek to destroy all the nations that come against Jerusalem" (Zechariah 12:9). The consequence for not standing with Jerusalem, the Jewish people, and for not being a blessing to them, is to be destroyed by God.

There is, however, one nation that had better not turn against Israel, Jerusalem, and the Jewish people. That is the ". . . Holy nation, His own special people, that you may proclaim the praises of Him who called you out of darkness into His marvelous light; who once were not a people but are now the people of God, who had not obtained mercy but now have obtained mercy" (1 Peter 2:9-10).

Isaiah also speaks to the nations, "For the nation and kingdom which will not serve you shall perish, and those nations shall be utterly ruined" (Isaiah 60:12). He is speaking about those not serving the Jewish people.

One of the most mystifying things yet to occur will be the families of the earth that will not go to Jerusalem to worship Jesus after He comes again. "And it shall come to pass that everyone who is left of all the nations which came against Jerusalem shall go up from year to year to worship the King, the LORD of hosts, and to keep the Feast of Tabernacles. And it shall be that whichever of the families of the earth do not come up to Jerusalem to worship the King, the LORD of hosts, on them there will be no rain. If the family of Egypt will not come up and enter in, they shall have no rain; they shall receive the plague with which the LORD strikes the nations who do not come up to keep the Feast of Tabernacles. This shall be the punishment of Egypt and the punishment of all the nations that do not come up to keep the Feast of Tabernacles" (Zechariah 14:16-19).

Which feasts do you, your family, or the congregation you attend, celebrate? Judaism is the root that supports you (Romans 11:18). What do you know about the feasts? Leviticus 23:1,2,4 say, "And the LORD spoke to Moses, saying, 'Speak to the children of Israel, and say to them: "The feasts of the LORD, which you shall proclaim to be holy convocations, these are My feasts. These are the feasts of the LORD, holy convocations which you shall proclaim at their appointed times".'"

It saddens me to see churches keep pagan holidays and know nothing about the feasts of the Lord from the Bible. Who is proclaiming and preparing the families now to go to Jerusalem to worship the King of Kings and celebrate the Feast of Tabernacles? Thank God for those who do; however, they are few and far between.

God wants to bless and not punish. It is up to us what we will receive.

REVERSE

Many books written have a Foreword. But I was impressed to include a "Reverse".

There have been times in my life when I have had to stop and back up. Sometimes it is because I have done the wrong thing, or I have sinned or disobeyed the Lord. These times are not easy, and no matter how long it takes, I have to stop what I am doing and go in reverse. Back to the Lord.

An example of this is found in the life of Abraham. In Genesis 12, God calls him to go to the land of Canaan. But because there is a famine there, Abraham continued on to Egypt. God never told him to go to Egypt, therefore, he missed the miracles the Lord would have done for him and his family.

In Genesis 13, Abraham stopped, went into reverse, and went back to the last ". . . place of the altar which he had made there at first. And there Abram called on the name of the LORD" (Genesis 13:4).

When I sin, my pride rises up and tries to prevent me from going back to the Lord, so I have to humble myself, repent, and go back to the last place I heard from the Lord. Then I can go forward again with His direction.

There is also another kind of Reverse. It is where we stop, back up, and reflect upon what the Lord is showing us. I pray that the readers of this book do precisely that. Pause and reflect about end-time evangelism and your part in it, or as is stated in the Book of Psalms, "Selah".

I thought about titling this Reverse, "In One Hour". Babylon will fall in one hour according to Revelation 18. I believe this to be one of the great end-time battles, and joining with the Lord to participate in it will be only for those who "are called, chosen, and faithful" (Revelation 17:14).

Another question to ask yourself: What will happen to the world's natural and economic conditions to cause the Jewish people to leave their nations and go to Israel, especially from the United States? And, what will be my role concerning that?

I hope this book confirms to some, what the Lord has already shown them. To others, that it will stir up and provoke their pure minds. And to still others, open them up to see what God is doing with and through the Jewish people and their return to Israel.

May the Lord bless you out of Zion!

Steve Lightle

ENDNOTES

1. *Newsweek, The International Newsmagazine,* January 22, 1990, page 16.

2. Australia, Argentina, Belgium, Bolivia, United Kingdom, Brazil, Canada, Chile, Columbia, Costa Rica, Cuba, Denmark, Dominican Republic, Ecuador, USA, France, Guatemala, Haiti, Honduras, Ireland, Mexico, Nicaragua, Norway, New Zealand, Panama, Paraguay, Netherlands, Peru, Sweden, Switzerland, Uruguay, Venezuela.

3. *While Six Million Died,* Arthur D. Morse, Random House, New York, 1967.

4. *Proceedings of the Intergovernmental Committee, Evian, July 6th to 15th, 1938, Verbatim Records of the Plenary Meetings of the Committee, Resolutions and Reports,* pp. 12-13.

5. Ibid., Summary of the Proceedings, page 18.

6. Ibid., page 9.

7. Ibid., page 12.

8. Ibid., page 15.

9. Ibid, page 16

ABOUT THE AUTHOR

Steve Lightle is a former businessman from Seattle, Washington, where he owned a restaurant and "Dippy Duck Car Wash". In June 1973, Steve moved his family to Braunschweig, West Germany, the city that gave Hitler his German citizenship.

In August 1974, he received a vision of God's plan to bring the Jewish people out from the then Soviet Union and return them to the Land of Israel.

From 1976 to 1981, Steve was the European Director of the Full Gospel Business Men's Fellowship International, based in Brussels, Belgium. He traveled and ministered extensively throughout Europe.

For two and one-half years, Steve worked together with Eastern European Bible Mission, working behind the Iron Curtain. He has made many trips to the former Soviet Union.

In 1982, Steve and his family moved to Jerusalem, Israel, where they lived for seven years.

In 1991, together with Gustav Scheller, he helped establish the Exodus Shipping Line to bring Jewish people from the USSR to Israel by ship and airplane.

In 1983, Steve wrote the book *EXODUS II*. Currently, he and his wife Judy live in Bellevue, Washington. He travels and speaks around the world.

APPENDIX 1

World Jewish Population

"The annual pre-Rosh Hashana study put the total number of Jews worldwide at about 13.5 million, with the U.S. home to 5.6 million. However, Israel, expected to have 4.9 million by the end of the coming Jewish year, will become the largest Jewish community within a few years, the report said.

USA	5,600,000
Israel	4,900,000
France	600,000
Russia	400,000
Canada	360,000
Ukraine	280,000
Great Britain	280,000
Argentina	220,000
Germany	70,000
Iran	25,000
Panama	7,000
Hong Kong	2,500

Jews today are found in more than 100 countries, the report said, a World Jewish Congress study."*

* *The Jerusalem Post*, North American Edition, September 26, 1998, front page.

APPENDIX 2

EXODUS II is not a nonprofit organization; therefore I have nothing to build.

I am but a voice. However, I do know organizations that are upright, truthful, and getting Jewish people to Israel, not spending large amounts of money on themselves. They are prayerfully responsible for the finances they receive.

If you are directed by the Lord to give money to help Jews go to Israel and would like to know where to send funds, you may contact us at:

> EXODUS II
> P.O. Box 70069
> Bellevue, WA 98007
> U.S.A.

We will forward your name and address on to those we know, or send their address to you if you prefer.

APPENDIX 3

During the Gulf War, or "Desert Storm" as it was called, I put together a 2-hour video of slides and explanations of the trip to Iraq. This video, "Revealing the Spirit of Babylon," shows pictures of the ten cities told about in Genesis 10 that Nimrod built. The video also contains scenes of the rebuilding of ancient Babylon by Saddam Hussein. In addition, it shows some other shocking things, i.e., where the idea of the Statue of Liberty came from. This video is available for $19.95 + $4.50 for shipping and handling, (U.S.) from:

EXODUS II
P.O. Box 70069
Bellevue, WA 98008-0069
U.S.A.